FATHER KNOWS BEST

*Words That Celebrate the World's
Most Wonderful Dads*

Edited and with an Introduction by David Lyon

THE LYONS PRESS
Guilford, Connecticut

An imprint of The Globe Pequot Press

Copyright © 2008 Morris Book Publishing, LLC

The Lyons Press is an imprint of The Globe Pequot Press.

Designed by Sheryl P. Kober

Library of Congress Cataloging-in-Publication Data
Father knows best : words that celebrate the world's most wonderful dads / edited and with an introduction by David Lyon.
    p. cm.
 Includes bibliographical references.
 ISBN 978-1-59921-249-4
 1. Fathers--Quotations. 2. Fatherhood--Quotations, maxims, etc. I. Lyon, David, 1949-
PN6084.F3F37 2008
306.874'2--dc22

2007049968

Printed in the United States of America

10 9 8 7 6 5 4 3 2

FATHER KNOWS BEST

To my own father, and the father-in-law I wish I'd known.

Contents

Introduction **ix**

Solid as a Mountain: Father **1**

A Mysterious State: Fatherhood **33**

Bringing Home the Bacon: Dad the Breadwinner **63**

Station-Wagon Realities: The Art of Fathering **83**

Frontier Justice: Dad the Disciplinarian **131**

Nothing Dearer: Fathers and Daughters **149**

A Nervous Breakdown into Innings: Dads and Sports **183**

Our Similarities Are Different: Fathers and Sons **201**

God's Gifts to Children: Grandfathers **243**

Look Her Straight in the Eyes: Wisdom from Dad **263**

Selected Biographical Notes **279**

Index **287**

Introduction

Homer Simpson, the Ur-dad of Matt Groening's animated sitcom *The Simpsons,* was probably on to something when he opined, "I won't lie to you—fatherhood isn't easy like motherhood." It was an audacious claim, given that Marge would hardly agree.

But in his own clueless way, Homer had a point—modern fatherhood is a mystery. For mothers, at least biology gives them a head start on their jobs as parents. But fathers have to make it up as they go along. As anthropologist Margaret Mead observed, "Fathers are biological necessities, but social accidents."

The ambiguity of fatherhood begins in our oldest myths. The original Bad Dad was Saturn, the Titan who devoured his own children so that they wouldn't topple him as ruler of the universe. But his youngest, Zeus, escaped and established a rather more upbeat image of fatherhood, giving birth to Athena from his own head and fathering a large brood of gods and goddesses and a veritable horde of mortals. What with his dalliances in the guise of a swan, a rain of gold, or a bull, Zeus wasn't exactly the ideal role model of a dad—as his wife, Hera, kept reminding him—but the mortal Greeks adored him. (He was, after all, every ancient Greek's answer to the question, "Who's your daddy?")

How the mighty have fallen! In a speech to the National Father's Day Committee in 1961, Adlai E. Stevenson observed that "especially since World War II, father has come upon sorry times. He is the butt of the comic strips; he is the boob of the radio and TV serials; and the favorite stooge of all our professional comedians."

Goodbye, Zeus. Hello, Homer Simpson.

For each bumbling dad on prime-time television there are tens of thousands more at home who show a real knack for fatherhood. Having kids transforms many men. As Muhammad Ali wisely said, "Children make you want to start life over." And many dads do exactly that. Sociological literature abounds with tales of men who straightened up and flew right once they became fathers, and Hollywood regularly churns out heartwarming stories of troubled, often lost men who suddenly become solid dads and good people once their children arrive.

The earth shifts. "The night you were born, I ceased being my father's boy and became my son's father," author Henry George Felson wrote to his son. "That night I began a new life."

Despite changes in the modern economy, fathers remain the principal breadwinners in four-fifths of American families, according to the U.S. Census. Their very absence is part of their authority. As Canadian author Margaret Atwood noted, "All fathers are invisible in daytime; daytime is ruled by mothers and fathers come out at night. Darkness brings home fathers, with their real, unspeakable power. There is more to fathers than meets the eye."

An old French proverb, "A father is a banker provided by Nature," suggests that the provider dad is nothing new. Yet the consequence of this arrangement in our spread-out country is the absence of the father from the home for most of the day—and much of the evening, too, if he has a long commute. "There's really no point in having children if you're not going to be home enough to father them," actor Anthony Edwards once said, perhaps echoing the wisdom of the Reverend Jesse Jackson, who is fond of telling parents, "Your children need your presence more than your presents."

Indeed, one of Dad's charges, at least in modern American society, is to instill a love of games into his sons and daughters. And many grown children recall those sporting interactions with a glow of fondness. "Baseball is fathers and sons playing catch, lazy and murderous, wild and controlled, the profound archaic song of birth, growth, age, and death," wrote poet Donald Hall. The father who does not press but joins his child in the game inculcates the greatest love for the sport. "To this day," Tiger Woods said when his father was still alive, "my dad has never asked me to go play golf. I ask him. It's the child's desire to play that matters, not the parent's desire to have the child play."

Most dads can't resist sharing what they consider to be nuggets of wisdom. One of the commonest phrases in conversation may be "As my father always used to tell me . . ." Even Shakespeare wasn't above a bit of fatherly advice. Some of the most famous lines of *Hamlet* are spoken by Polonius to his son, Laertes: "This above all: to thine own self be true, and it must follow, as the night the day, thou canst not then be false to any man."

Of course, what Dad doesn't say may be the most important of all. "My father used to say that we must surrender our youth to purchase wisdom," Australian novelist Morris West once recalled. "What he never told me was how badly we get cheated on the exchange rate."

For better or worse, Dear Old Dad is also often cast as lawgiver and disciplinarian. When he shouts "You're not leaving the house dressed like that, young lady!" he probably means it, even if he has to repeat it so often that he's likely to resort to the old parental chestnut, "If I've told you once, I've told you a thousand times."

Yet ferocity has fallen from favor as an attribute for dads. A few generations ago, Lord Mountbatten could assert, "My father was afraid of his father, I was afraid of my father, and I don't see why my children shouldn't be afraid of me." Nowadays, most dads would more happily concur with Henry Wadsworth Longfellow: "A torn jacket is soon mended, but hard words bruise the heart of a child."

Conversely, few fathers ever regret kind words. History knows Sigmund Freud as a complex and inscrutable man, but he was different with his daughter. "My father praised me and comforted me," wrote Anna Freud. "That made me so happy that nothing else mattered."

Skipping a generation lets men indulge their warmest sides as grandfathers. As politician Rudolph Giuliani once pointed out, "What children need most are the essentials that grandparents provide in abundance. They give unconditional love, kindness, patience, humor, comfort, lessons in life. And, most importantly, cookies."

Cookies—even Homer Simpson could agree with that.

Solid as a Mountain: Father

Let us now praise famous men, and our fathers
that begat us.

—Sirach 44:1,
King James Bible

**Becoming a father isn't difficult, but it's
very difficult to be a father.**

—Wilhelm Busch

It's all any reasonable child can expect
if the dad is present at the conception.

—Joe Orton

The years lived by our father before he begot us have upon them a wonder that cannot easily be matched. Just as we feel ourselves half participant in the experiences of our children, so in some dim way do we share in those adventures of this mortal who not so long ago moved over the face of the earth like a god to call us up from the deep.

—Llewelyn Powys

Fathers are biological necessities, but social accidents.

–Margaret Mead

surprise!
According to the U.S. Department of Commerce, the most popular Father's Day gift is a
necktie.

I wish either my father or my mother, or indeed both of them, as they were in duty both equally bound to it, had minded what they were about when they begot me.

—Laurence Sterne, Tristram Shandy

When you played make-believe as a child,
you probably played at being a cop, a robber,
a cowboy, an Indian, a Jedi warrior, or a home-
run slugger about ten thousand times. But how
many times did you pretend to be a daddy?

—Kevin Osborn
The Complete Idiot's Guide to Fatherhood

Why are men reluctant to become fathers?
They aren't through being
children.

—Cindy Garner

Sherman made the terrible discovery that men make about their fathers sooner or later…that the man before him was not an aging father but a boy … who grew up and had a child of his own and, as best he could, out of a sense of duty and, perhaps love, adopted a role called Being a Father so that his child would have something mythical and infinitely important: a Protector. . . .

—Tom Wolfe
Bonfire of the Vanities

THE CHILD IS FATHER OF THE MAN.

—WILLIAM WORDSWORTH

When a man learns that he is going to be a father, it's a moment of such great impact that he'll remember it forever.

–Quinton Skinner

Blessed indeed is the man who hears many gentle voices call him father!

—Lydia Maria Child

It is easier for a father to have children than for children to have a real father.

—Pope John Paul XXIII

There is no good father, that's the rule. Don't lay the blame on men but on the bond of paternity, which is rotten. To beget children, nothing better; to *have* them, what iniquity!

—Jean-Paul Sartre

A father provides us with some of the most important life lessons of all. He can be a friend, a disciplinarian, a nurturing parent, a seemingly endless well of experience, our greatest enemy, and our greatest hero. **Oftentimes, he can be all of these things at once.**

—Larry King

Children want to feel instinctively that their father is behind them as solid as a mountain, but like a mountain, is something to look up to.

—Dorothy Thompson

AT BOTTOM GOD IS NOTHING OTHER THAN AN EXALTED FATHER.

—Sigmund Freud

My Mother always deferred to my Father, and in his absence spoke of him to me, as if he were all-wise. I confused him in some sense with God; at all events I believed that my Father knew every-thing and saw everything.

—Edmund Gosse
Father and Son

DIRECTLY AFTER GOD IN HEAVEN COMES PAPA.

—Wolfgang Amadeus Mozart

Old father, old artificer, stand me now and ever in good stead.

—Stephen Daedelus in *A Portrait of the Artist as a Young Man* by James Joyce

PROLIFIC POPS

According to the U.S. Census Bureau, research shows that fathers with the most offspring are, on average, nearly six years older than their wives.

The quest for the perfect father has thus far ended only in Heaven, but many fathers have assumed that their paternal efforts have assured them a place there.

—Alan Valentine

Life was a lot simpler when what we honored was father and mother rather than all major credit cards.

—Robert Orben

FATHER! — TO GOD HIMSELF WE CANNOT GIVE A HOLIER NAME.

—WILLIAM WORDSWORTH

The young need old men. They need men who are not ashamed of age, not pathetic imitations of themselves. . . . Parents are the bones on which children sharpen their teeth.

—Peter Ustinov
Dear Me

You don't have to deserve your mother's love. You have to deserve your father's.

—Robert Frost

There is something ultimate in a father's love, something that cannot fail, something to be believed against the whole world. We almost attribute practical omnipotence to our father in the days of our childhood.

—FREDERICK W. FABER, *Bethlehem*

Dad is every child's first idea of what a man is like—a son's image of what he may become, a daughter's first view of what she'll have to cope with.

—S. Adams Sullivan
The Father's Almanac

People see Archie Bunker everywhere. Particularly girls—poor girls, rich girls, all kinds of girls are always coming up to me and telling me that Archie is just like their dad.

—CARROLL O'CONNOR ON THE CHARACTER
HE PORTRAYED ON *All in the Family*

My dad always set a good example for us—we learned so much just by watching how he did things, and we could tell he held us to some pretty high standards in terms of working hard, being knowledgeable and prepared, understanding the people around us, keeping organized, and taking what we do seriously.

—Bill Gates

Most fathers are unaware how important even the simplest actions can be. The way we take off our shoes and hang our coat, the way we store our tools or open our briefcase, all make a lasting impression on our children.

—Jack Petrash
Covering Home

One father is more than a hundred schoolmasters.

—George Herbert

If parents would only realize how they bore their children.

—George Bernard Shaw

Experientia does it—as Papa used to say.

—Charles Dickens
David Copperfield

I'm not going to buy my kids an encyclopedia. Let them walk to school like I did.

—Yogi Berra

♛

Jarrell was not so much a father . . . as an affectionate encyclopedia.

—MARY JARRELL ON HER HUSBAND RANDALL JARRELL

♛

I believe that what we become depends on what our fathers teach us at odd moments, when they aren't trying to teach us.

—Umberto Eco

Dad's Other Obligations

Under the federal Family and Medical Leave Act, dads as well as moms are allowed a total of twelve work weeks per year of unpaid leave from their jobs to tend to a child's birth, adoption, or acceptance into foster care, or to care for an immediate family member with a serious health condition.

I have never been jealous. Not even when my dad finished fifth grade a year before I did.

–Jeff Foxworthy

♛

The nurturing father is not the product of recent times, but is a man whose feelings of self-esteem are as invested in his children and his ability to be a loving parent as in his work and career. Although this type of man is in the minority, he has always been around.

—Louis Genevie, PhD, and Eva Margolies, *The Motherhood Report*

[M]any fathers do not realize the importance of their own contributions to a child's development. . . . By causing children to laugh, cry, think and love, fathers provide the most precious of memories to savor and to celebrate.

—Mary Kay Shanley

[H]is speech was a perfectly intelligent speech about fathers not being dispensable and nobody agreed with that more than I did.

—Candice Bergen on Vice President Dan Quayle's remark that her TV character Murphy Brown was "mocking the importance of fathers by bearing a child alone"

There was a time when father amounted to something in the United States. He was held with some esteem in the community; he had some authority in his own household; his views were sometimes taken seriously by his children; and even his wife paid heed to him from time to time.

In recent years, however, especially since World War II, father has come upon sorry times. He is the butt of the comic strips; he is the boob of the radio and TV serials; and the favorite stooge of all our professional comedians.

—ADLAI E. STEVENSON

The father in contemporary TV ads never knows what cold medicine to take. And in situation comedies, *The Cosby Show* notwithstanding, men are devious, bumbling, or easy to outwit. It is the women who outwit them, and teach them a lesson, or hold the whole town together all by themselves.

—Robert Bly
Iron John

WHEN ONE HAS NOT HAD A GOOD FATHER, ONE MUST CREATE ONE.

—FRIEDRICH WILHELM NIETZSCHE

We criticize mothers for closeness. We criticize fathers for distance. How many of us have expected less from our fathers and appreciated what they gave us more? How many of us always let them off the hook?

—Ellen Goodman

Fathers should be neither seen nor heard. That is the only proper basis for family life.

—Oscar Wilde
An Ideal Husband

Mothers have been wondering about this forever. There you are, having given this baby valuable real estate right next to your internal organs for nine months . . . and then the kid gets born, and once she's looking around for something to name, the something she picks is "Dada."

—Sandi Kahn Shelton

Be kind to thy father, for when thou wert young, who loved thee so fondly as he? He caught the first accents that fell from thy tongue, and joined in thy innocent glee.

—Margaret Courtney

All the feeling which my father could not put into words was in his hand—any dog, child, or horse would recognize the kindness of it.

—Freya Stark

I hope you will always be able to say in after life that you had a kind father.

–Charles Dickens to his youngest son

All fathers are invisible in daytime; daytime is ruled by mothers and fathers come out at night. Darkness brings home fathers, with their real, unspeakable power. There is more to fathers than meets the eye.

—Margaret Atwood

He opened the jar of pickles when no one else could. He was the only one in the house who wasn't afraid to go into the basement by himself. He cut himself shaving, but no one kissed it or got excited about it. It was understood when it rained, he got the car and brought it around to the door. When anyone was sick, he went out to get the prescription filled. **He took lots of pictures . . . but he was never in them.**

—Erma Bombeck

A good father is one of the most unsung, unpraised, unnoticed, and yet one of the most valuable assets in our society.

—Billy Graham

In spite of the great difference between the Roman pater-familias, whose family was his property, and the modern father, the feeling that children are brought into the world to satisfy the parents and to compensate them for the disappointments of their own lives is still widespread.

—Erich Fromm
Man for Himself

The family has been regarded as a small State of which the husband and father is head.

—Havelock Ellis

My grandfather is the king, my dad's the prince, I guess that makes me the butler.

—Adam Petty

No man is responsible for his father. That is entirely his mother's affair.

—Margaret Turnbull

The fundamental defect of fathers is that they want their children to be a credit to them.

—Bertrand Russell

For 5,000 years, fathers have passed their skills so their sons can be farmers, soldiers, accountants, dentists, and doctors. When a father smiles, "I am so proud of my son, he is just like me," remember, dad is praising himself.

—David Cohen

The odds are that . . . you've experienced situations in which your words or feelings at work reminded you of an encounter with your father. People commonly report talking to a subordinate exactly how their fathers talked to them, even to the point of using the same expressions. They also frequently recall relating to a boss in the same way that they related to their father.

—Stephan B. Poulter, PhD
The Father Factor

You have to dig deep to

bury your daddy.

—Gypsy proverb

It is impossible to please all the world and one's father.

—Jean de La Fontaine

Don't hold your parents up to contempt.
After all, you are their son, and it is just
possible that you may take after them.

—Evelyn Waugh

Perhaps there is a distance that is the optimum distance for seeing one's father, farther than across the supper table or across the room, somewhere in the middle distance: He is dwarfed by trees or the sweep of a hill, but his features are still visible, his body language still distinct.

—Jane Smiley
A Thousand Acres

NO ONE LIKE ONE'S MOTHER AND FATHER EVER LIVED.

—Robert Lowell

What I learned is that if I don't know something, I just shrug my shoulders and admit it. Doctors don't know everything. Neither do teachers. Or dads.

—Frank McCourt

LIFE DOESN'T COME WITH AN INSTRUCTION BOOK—THAT'S WHY WE HAVE FATHERS.

—H. JACKSON BROWN

A Mysterious State:
Fatherhood

No man can possibly know what life means, what the world means, what anything means, until he has a child and loves it. And then the whole universe changes and nothing will ever again seem exactly as it seemed before.

—Lafcadio Hearn

Like anything worthwhile, fatherhood can be difficult, test our limits and is short on easy answers. Fatherhood is also the most rewarding activity a man can undertake in his life.

—Michael Horowitz, PhD

Most of us become parents long before we have stopped being children.

—Mignon McLaughlin

The new father ... feels that his mere impregnation of his mate, done every day by otters and apes, is Olympic gold medal stuff.

—Bill Cosby
On Fatherhood

While Hillary was in the recovery room, I carried Chelsea out to Mother and anyone else who was available to see the world's most wonderful baby. I talked to her and sang to her. I never wanted that night to end. At last I was a father. Despite my love for politics and government and my growing ambitions, I knew then that being a father was the most important job I'd ever have.

—Bill Clinton

Fatherhood for me started when my daughter, Neve, was born. . . . Immediately after the birth, the doctor handed me some scissors and told me to cut the umbilical cord. . . . It seemed like an odd time to start someone off on surgical training. But we men are task-oriented, so it was probably the doctor's way of keeping me from passing out.

—Conan O'Brien

Even though it has come to be a sort of routine for me, I am stirred and moved and **filled with happiness every time.**

—Leo Tolstoy, on birth of his ninth child

I looked at that kid for a long time. I felt something impossible for me to explain. Then it came to me—I was a father.

—Nat King Cole

Literature is mostly about having sex and not much about having children. Life is the other way around.

–David Lodge

Thirteen, thirteen children, and I love—**I love them all.** And I think I've been a good father to all of them.

—Anthony Quinn

I did not expect to cry when my son was born—it seemed a silly and conventional and trivial thing to do, weep for joy, like a figure in an advertisement—but I did, quite suddenly and without warning, as if it were a reflex.

—Alec Wilkinson

Fatherhood has been known to transform even the toughest and most resilient into a quivering mass.

–Marcus Jacob Goldman
The Joy of Fatherhood

I kind of cuddled him like a football.

—Quarterback Tom Brady on first holding his son

The night you were born, I ceased being my father's boy and became my son's father. That night I began a new life.

—HENRY GEORGE FELSON

Remembering Dad

According to the U.S. Census Bureau, Americans give slightly more than 100 million Father's Day cards each year, but only half of them are purchased specifically by sons or daughters.

People talk about the emotions that come when
a baby is born: exuberance, relief, giddiness, pure
ecstasy. . . . I knew I was supposed to be feeling all
of those things, and of course I did. But the domi-
nant emotion inside me was a more basic one.
I was scared; scared of what I knew was sure to
come, and more scared about what I didn't know.

—Bob Greene

Fatherhood was a mysterious state
and didn't seem to become any less so with time
and familiarity. At night, when I looked in on my
sleeping daughters, I would feel a deep sense of
improbability mingled with inadequacy.

—Geoffrey Norman

It became clear to me immediately when my son was born . . . that I could kill if anything was going to happen to him. If somebody wasn't putting the thermostat on the right temperature there in the hospital, I could kill that person. It's a strange, new feeling of wanting to protect this young man at all costs.

—Jon Stewart

I came to understand that you have to **practice at being a good father** and practice at being a good husband, **just as you have to practice at being a good journalist.**

—Bob Schieffer

I'm just as insufferable and useless as every other dad is. The dynamic never changes, no matter what you do for a living.

–Glenn Frey

What a terrific deal. Without lifting a finger, without even being big, and whether or not we deserve it, we are automatically looked up to, respected, possibly worshipped. Because our kids have to look up to us in the simplest physical sense, they look up to us in other ways as well.

— S. Adams Sullivan

The generative transformation of selfish men abruptly thrown into unavoidable close contact with young children is an enduring kind of Cinderella story that has formed the plot of a surprisingly large number of recent Hollywood movies.

—Katherine Ellison

[B]EING A FATHER IS LESS ABOUT WHAT A MAN *does* THAN WHO HE *is*.

—MARK O'CONNELL, PhD

[W]ise men have always recognized that of all professions fatherhood is the most demanding and the least apprenticed. The fine art of paternity must be learned from experience that usually brings its wisdom too late.

—Alan Valentine

👑

I was the same kind of father as I was a harpist—I played by ear.

—Harpo Marx

Ideally, they should give you a couple of "practice kids" before you have any for real. Sort of like bowling a few frames for free before you start keeping score. Let you warm up.

—Paul Reiser
Couplehood

I'm gonna be the best dad that ever lived. I'll have a ranch with a race car track and a golf course.

—Jeremy London

I wasn't anything special as a father. But I loved them, and they knew it.

–Sammy Davis, Jr.

When your kid is born you can still be perfect. You haven't made any mistakes yet.

—GIL BUCKMAN, PLAYED BY STEVE MARTIN
IN THE MOVIE *Parenthood*

[T]he standards for fatherhood are so uncertain, it seems that children would be well within their rights to ask of their parents, "So who put you in charge?"

—Mark O'Connell, PhD

I won't lie to you—fatherhood isn't easy like motherhood.

— HOMER J. SIMPSON, ANIMATED DAD OF
MATT GROENING'S *The Simpsons*

I can be a good father, but I'm a terrible mother.

—Prince Rainier of Monaco

A king, realizing his incompetence, can either delegate or abdicate his duties. A father can do neither. If only sons could see the paradox, they would understand the dilemma.

—Marlene Dietrich

It's the most fun I've ever had and also the biggest pain . . . I've ever experienced.

–Brad Pitt on fatherhood

The most noticeable change in me since I became a parent is that I've loosened up. I sing Elmo songs at the top of my lungs as I'm driving down the highway. When I'm with my son in a crowd of people and Wiggles are in front of us, I'm much more willing to do the Wiggles dance.

—Matt Lauer

[Fatherhood] is a little indescribable, like trying to explain a guitar chord to somebody. I can just say that it broadens your world and deepens the things that you feel. It's a really wonderful feeling.

—Matt Damon

CHILDren make you want to start Life over.

—Muhammad Ali

Of course if you like your kids, if you love them from the moment they begin, you yourself begin all over again, in them, with them, and so there is something more to the world again.

—William Saroyan

In order to discover your children, you have to sort of come to terms with yourself. When you start looking at life through the lens of a three-year-old, it's like your whole filter changes. Everything you look at is like a painting that's been restored. Everything is alive again, because you just don't take it for granted.

—Andre Agassi

BEING A FATHER HELPS ME BE MORE RESPONSIVE. . . . YOU SEE MORE THINGS THAN YOU'VE EVER SEEN.

—KID ROCK

[Fatherhood] has been great. All your priorities change. I definitely work a lot less. . . . Even when she is sleeping, I am like, let me make a noise and wake her up, just so I can hang with her a few more minutes. **My wife hates that.**

—Adam Sandler

I think I was on my way to being a different kind of parent anyway, but now I don't have to give lectures about persistence and resilience and doing things in spite of challenges. The [Parkinson's disease] gives me a certain authority.

—Michael J. Fox

My greatest achievement, I think, has been being a successful parent, sending my kids to school. They are all college grads. They understand who they are, where they are, and have made a good statement with their lives. I think that has been the best thing that I have done.

—Kareem Abdul-Jabbar

There's so much negative imagery of black fatherhood. I've got tons of friends that are doing the right thing by their kids, and doing the right thing as a father—**and how come that's not as newsworthy?**

—Will Smith

I don't care what they say about me when I'm through with sports. I don't want to be known as anything else in life but a great father.

—Deion Sanders

Hey, my baby fetches me beer, and she's only four months old! Yeah, I'm a proud dad!

–James Hetfield

[A]s soon as I walk in the front door and into the living room, Amanda sees me and starts screaming and laughing. . . . It makes me feel like I'm the Beatles getting off an airplane.

—Bob Greene

Being a father, being a friend, those are the things that make me feel successful.

—William Hurt

There are to us no ties at all just in being a father. A son is distinctly an acquired taste. It's the practice of parenthood that makes you feel that, after all, there may be something in it.

—Heywood Broun

A Day OF HIS Own

The first Father's Day was proclaimed in Spokane, Washington, in 1910. The first presidential proclamation of Father's Day was made in 1966 by President Lyndon B. Johnson. It has been celebrated annually on the third Sunday of June since 1972, when President Richard M. Nixon signed a public law to make it a permanent observance.

It is a delight above all delights to see one's children turn out—as ours have done—all that the heart covets in children; and my delight is so full that I sometimes fancy my heart will have to burst for its own relief.

—Henry James, Sr.

Nothing affords me greater pleasure than to gratify the reasonable desires of my children, especially when they evince a disposition to promote the happiness of their parents, by diligent improvement of their time and talents, and uniform attention to those rules of morality which adorn the human character.

—Stephen Longfellow to his son
Henry Wadsworth Longfellow

When I was a boy, I used to do what my father wanted. Now I have to do what my boy wants. My problem is: When am I going to do what I want?

—Sam Levenson

There are times when parenthood seems nothing but feeding the mouth that bites you.

—Peter De Vries

Like any father, I have moments when I wonder whether I belong to the children or they belong to me.

—Bob Hope

Our three young children are all in Switzerland, the older boy in Munich, and my wife and I are like middle-aged omnibus-horses let loose in a pasture. The first time we have had a holiday together for fifteen years; I feel like a barrel without hoops!

—William James

By profession I am a soldier and take great pride in that fact, but I am also prouder, infinitely prouder, to be a father. A soldier destroys in order to build; the father only builds, never destroys.

—Douglas MacArthur

That's the interesting thing about becoming a father. Suddenly you universally have something in common with other people. I can be sitting next to a very straight, humorless businessman or stockbroker type on an airplane, and we'll just start talking about kids. And that conversation lasts three or four hours.

—Johnny Depp

The principles of fatherhood are, in many ways, the principles of masculine mastery.

—Mark O'Connell, PhD

TRUE MATURITY IS ONLY REACHED WHEN A MAN REALIZES HE HAS BECOME A FATHER FIGURE TO HIS DAUGHTER'S GIRLFRIENDS— AND HE ACCEPTS IT.

—LARRY McMURTRY

[B]ecoming a father makes us think about our own childhood and our parents. We begin to understand them in ways that were never before possible. And we begin to have more sympathy for their faults and failings—those sins that might have seemed unforgivable when we were sixteen.

—Quinton Skinner

By the time a man realizes that maybe his father was right, he usually has a son who thinks he's wrong.

—Charles Wadsworth

Nothing I've ever done has given me more joys and rewards than being a father to my children.

—BILL COSBY

Your children are not your children. They are the sons and daughters of Life's longing for itself.

—Kahlil Gibran

I OUGHT TO BE SHOT.

—Oliva Donne, on becoming
father of quintuplets in 1934

If I have any more kids, the
**Planned Parenthood's gonna come picket
my house.**

—Geraldo Rivera

He wants to live on through something—and
in his case, his masterpiece is his son. . . . All
of us want that, and it gets more poignant as
we get more anonymous in this world.

—Arthur Miller on the character of Willy Loman in *Death of a Salesman*

How pleasant it is for a father to sit at his child's board. It is like an aged man reclining under the shadow of an oak he has planted.

—Sir Walter Scott

It is a grim old world, and I think one has need of children to keep one's faith clear and one's hope bright. One cannot think too evilly of a world in which one's sons and daughters are to live. For their sake, one must try not only to make it better but to make it good.

—Oscar W. Firkins

Bringing Home the Bacon:
Dad the Breadwinner

The American father... passes his life entirely on Wall Street and communicates with his family once a month by means of a telegram in cipher.

—Oscar Wilde

When I was a small child, I missed my father when he went to his office, especially on weekends.... Now, as a parent myself, I see more clearly his deep sense of responsibility, the integrity in his commitment to making sure his children started off with a solid foundation.

—Rebecca Walker

To be sure, working—that is, earning a living—is one aspect of fathering. It's one means that the father has of extending protection to his family. But it's *just* one. If he concentrates on this to the exclusion of other aspects, it becomes not a form of fathering, **but an escape.**

—Myron Brenton

IT IS CLEAR THAT MOST AMERICAN CHILDREN SUFFER FROM TOO MUCH MOTHER AND TOO LITTLE FATHER.

—GLORIA STEINEM

Father, dear father, come home with me now,
The clock in the belfry strikes one;
You said you were coming right home from the shop
As soon as your day's work was done.

—Henry Clay Work

OFF TO WORK

Fathers are the principal bread-winners in 80 percent of American households, according to the U.S. Census Bureau.

Please be patient with
an extremely busy father.
–Walter Annenberg

It used to be that a penis could buy a person a lot of down-time. People who had them got to go away to a mysterious "office" every day and then come home and demand rest afterwards, on the theory that this "office" had gotten them so worn out and grouchy that they could hardly be expected to help with such things as dinner preparations, small children, and dog shit on the rug.

— Sandi Kahn Shelton

I wanted to be a forest ranger or a coal man. At a very early age, I knew I didn't want to do what my dad did, which was work in an office.

—Harrison Ford

Daddy's Gotta Bring Home the Bacon.

—Ted Kramer, played by Dustin Hoffman
in the movie *Kramer vs Kramer*

There is absolutely no excuse for a parent to abdicate his most important duty—the proper raising of his children. No father should be allowed to get away with the cowardly logic which concludes that his only job in the family is to pay for the bacon.

—Adlai E. Stevenson

[N]ow the money I make is earmarked for taking care of Amanda. I know I'm not the only new father who feels this way; a man the other day told me that for the first time in his life he was lying awake at night wondering if he had enough money stashed away. The reason was that he has a new daughter.

—Bob Greene

THERE'S REALLY NO POINT IN HAVING CHILDREN IF YOU'RE NOT GOING TO BE HOME ENOUGH TO FATHER THEM.

—Anthony Edwards

I wasn't really aware that my father was working for quite a while. I thought that it was my mother who had all the money.

—Peter Fonda

I wish I could have been a better father when my children were growing up, and less frightened about my own future, and how I was going to make a living, so I could have spent more real attention on them.

–Hal Holbrook

I AM A BIT OF AN ABSENT FATHER BECAUSE OF MY PROFESSION AND MY TRAVEL SCHEDULES, AND THERE'S A GUILT.

—MIKHAIL BARYSHNIKOV

YOU HAVE A LIFETIME TO WORK, BUT CHILDREN ARE ONLY YOUNG ONCE.

—POLISH PROVERB

I look at my father, who was in many ways an unhappy person, but who, not long before he got sick, said that the greatest source of satisfaction in his life had been going to work in the company of other workers.

—Jonathan Franzen

My father used to rehearse us so much, he just became the boss. Now I can see I was blessed. He would be so tired from working in that steel mill that we kids knew we only had a couple of hours to hang with him before he fell asleep.

—Bobby Womack

As I've participated in men's gatherings since the early 1980s, I've heard one statement over and over from American males, which has been phrased in a hundred different ways: "There is not enough father."

—Robert Bly

I grew up with the white picket fence. My dad went to work nine to five, and he had a station wagon.

—Matt Dillon

Hard work, ambition, and achievement are learned behaviors in families. The odds are that if you're highly successful, so, too, was your father and his father before him.

—Stephan B. Poulter, PhD
The Father Factor

My father taught me to work; he did not teach me to love it. I never did like to work, and I don't deny it. I'd rather read, tell stories, crack jokes, talk—anything but work.

—Abraham Lincoln

I don't fill the house with trophies, my home is as normal as possible, and my kids see me as just Dad who goes racing.

—Peter Brock

What is a normal childhood? We weren't rich, we were pretty middle class. My dad survived from job to job; with him taking care of so many relatives, he couldn't save any money.

—Charlie Sheen

That is the thankless position of the father in the family—the provider for all, and the enemy of all.

—August Strindberg

A Father is a Banker Provided by Nature.

—French proverb

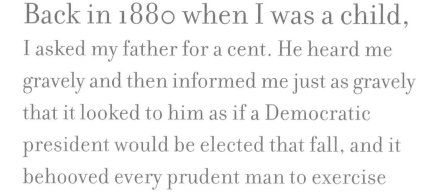

Back in 1880 when I was a child, I asked my father for a cent. He heard me gravely and then informed me just as gravely that it looked to him as if a Democratic president would be elected that fall, and it behooved every prudent man to exercise especial thrift. Therefore, he would be obliged to deny my request.

—Calvin Coolidge

My hair stands on end at the costs and charges of these boys. Why was I ever a father! Why was my father ever a father!

—Charles Dickens

I enclose $1.00. Spend it liberally, generously, carefully, judiciously, sensibly. Get from it pleasure, wisdom, health, and experience.

–Edward Fitzgerald to his son F. Scott Fitzgerald

Providing for one's family as a good husband and father is a watertight excuse for making money hand over fist. Greed may be a sin, exploitation of other people, might, on the face of it, look rather nasty, but who can blame a man for "doing the best" for his children?

—Eva Figes

My father made a million or two as a businessman and inventor and lost it all in the '29 crash . . . and told his five kids to laugh with him about it.

—Telly Savalas

He who is taught to live upon little owes more to his father's wisdom than he who has a great deal left him does to his father's care.

—William Penn

Where I come from, you don't really talk about how much you're earning. Those things are private. My dad never told my mum how much he was earning. I'm certainly not going to tell the world.

—PAUL MCCARTNEY

There has been a succession of women's revolutions in America. But watch out for the revolt of the father, if he should get fed up with feeding others, and get bored with being used, and lay down his tools, and walk off to consult his soul.

—Max Lerner

Mother Nature, in her infinite wisdom, has instilled within each of us a powerful biological instinct to reproduce; this is her way of assuring that the human race, come what may, **will never have any disposable income.**

—Dave Barry

I can always count on getting one thing for Father's Day—all the bills from Mother's Day.

—Milton Berle

It doesn't make any difference how much money a father earns, his name is always Dad-Can-I; and he always wonders whether these little people were born to beg.

—Bill Cosby
Fatherhood

A child, like your stomach, doesn't need all you can afford to give it.

—Frank A. Clark

Your children need your presence more than your presents.

—The Reverend Jesse Jackson

Sometimes the poorest man leaves
his children the richest inheritance.

—Ruth E. Renkel

No one on his deathbed ever said, "I wish
I had spent more time on my business."

—Paul Tsongas

COST OF KIDS

According to the U.S. Department of Agriculture, a family can expect to spend more than $165,000 to raise a child to age eighteen.

Station-Wagon Realities: The Art of Fathering

Before I got married, I had six theories about bringing up children; now I have six children and no theories.

—John Wilmot

☗

As a group, human fathers are models of paternal care, compared to roughly 90 percent of the mammal world, in which the standard is for dads to say "Ciao!" after conception.

—Katherine Ellison
The Mommy Brain

If the new American father feels bewildered and even defeated, let him take comfort from the fact that whatever he does in any fathering situation has a 50 percent chance of being right. . . . There are no absolutes in raising children. In any stressful situation, fathering is always a roll of the dice. The game may be messy, but I have never found one with more rewards and joys.

—Bill Cosby

Except that right side up is best, there is not much to learn about holding a baby. There are 152 distinctly different ways—and all are right! At least all will do.

—Heywood Broun

The more people have studied different methods of bringing up children, the more they have come to the conclusion that what good mothers and fathers instinctively feel like doing for their babies is the best after all.

—Dr. Benjamin Spock
Dr. Spock's Baby and Child Care

Spread the diaper in the position of the diamond with you at bat. Then, fold second base down to home and set the baby on the pitcher's mound. Put first base and third together, bring up home plate and pin the three together. Of course, in case of rain, you gotta call the game and start all over again.

—Jimmy Piersall on how to diaper a baby

Of all the ingredients of successful father-hood, unselfish affection seems to be the most precious. Without it all paternal systems, all wisdom, and all sacrifices are likely to be futile. With it, a father may make innumerable blunders and still end his days warmed by filial love and pater-nal pride.

—Alan Valentine

My sense of my son as an enigma was reinforced during the first year because there was little I could provide for him. So far as I could tell, he liked dimly lit rooms, tranquil surroundings, breast milk, **and the company of his mother.**

—Alec Wilkinson

GOING IT ALONE

The number of single fathers raising children has more than tripled from 1970, according to the U.S. Census Bureau. About 2.3 million single parents living with their children are men.

The most important thing a father can do for his children is to love their mother.

—Theodore M. Hesburgh

Dad needs to show an incredible amount of respect and humor and friendship toward his mate so the kids understand their parents are sexy, they're fun, they do things together, they're best friends. Kids learn by example. If I respect Mom, they're going to respect Mom.

—Tim Allen

When the father is a supportive figure and a good parent, the family tends to be more cohesive and the mother is able to give more love and be more patient with her children. Mothers also feel better about themselves, their children, and motherhood in general.

—Louis Genevie, PhD, and Eva Margolies
The Motherhood Report

To be a successful father there's one absolute rule: when you have a kid, don't look at it for the first two years.

—Ernest Hemingway

I think the passion many people affect for children is merely a fashionable pose. I have a notion that children are all the better for not being burdened with too much parental love.

—W. Somerset Maugham

He didn't come out of my belly, but my God, I've made his bones, because I've attended to every meal, and how he sleeps, and the fact that he swims like a fish because I took him to the ocean. I'm so proud of all those things. But he is my biggest pride.

—John Lennon on his son Sean

The most important thing in my father's life? Me and my brother. My mom.

—Sean Lennon

He was like a real dad, you know. We used to sit down with guitars and mess around.

—Julian Lennon

The kind of man who thinks that helping with the dishes is beneath him will also think that helping with the baby is beneath him, and then he certainly is not going to be a very successful father.

—Eleanor Roosevelt

It used to be that the first real one-on-one involvement for many dads was teaching the kid to ride a two-wheeler on a Saturday afternoon, or, in some cases, sharing a six-pack sometime after college. If you're looking for an action-packed, me-and-you-as-pals kind of relationship, then the Brand New Baby is going to seem a little boring.

—Sandi Kahn Shelton

Today is Father's Day. If Dad is lucky, Mom will take over for him. Perhaps . . . he'll be excused from fixing formula, giving bottles, washing the dinner dishes, helping with homework, supervising the young-sters' baths, and getting them off to bed. Maybe . . . Mom and the children will take him out to dinner.

—Dorothy Barclay

Taking care of a newborn baby means devoting yourself, body and soul, twenty-four hours a day, seven days a week, to the welfare of someone whose major response, in the way of positive reinforce-ment, is to throw up on you.

—Dave Barry

Babies are always more trouble than you thought—and more wonderful.

—Charles Osgood

Everybody knows about the physical demands of motherhood. But with all due respect, once the baby's a year old, **fatherhood is the Ironman Triathlon.** It's Dad who carries the kids to the car, Dad who rides the roller coaster, **Dad who does piggyback.**

—Hugh O'Neill

In our society leaving baby with Daddy is just one step above leaving the kids to be raised by wolves or apes.

—Al Roker

It is with rare great pleasure that I see the preservation of children has become the care of men of sense. In my opinion this business has been left too fatally long to the management of women who cannot be supposed to have a proper knowledge to fit them for the task, notwithstanding they look upon it as their own province.

—William Cadogan
***Essay on Nursing*, 1764**

I have never liked it when a pen leaks on my shirt, or a newspaper smudges my pants. I'm far from a snappy dresser, but I don't like to dirty up my clothes. When I hold Amanda, though, and she's just eaten, and she spits up on the shoulder of my shirt—which she invariably does—it doesn't matter to me at all.

—Bob Greene

Let a father strap on a baby, and instantly there are people lined up to praise him for his involvement with his kid and to suggest that perhaps he is tired and couldn't they please help him by changing the child's poopy diaper while he relaxes with a beer.

—Sandi Kahn Shelton

Men encourage their babies' curiosity and, more specifically, encourage them actively to solve physical and intellectual challenges.

—Dr. Kyle Pruett

♛

While moms tend to pick comfortable activities that they know their babies can master, dads like to expand their babies' horizons by nudging them to learn new skills and experience new adventures.

—Susan Fox

I started reading when I was about three, a little over three. My father felt it was best if we did our own reading. He said he had too many things he wanted to read himself to waste his time reading to us. He said, "You want to read? Learn to read." He said, "Hell, you learned to walk at two years. You can certainly learn to read at three."

—CHUCK JONES

MY FATHER FELT THAT CHILDREN SHOULD MAKE THEIR OWN WAY.

—RON REAGAN

We think of a father as an old, or at least a middle-aged man. The astounding truth is that most fathers are young men, and that they make their greatest sacrifices in their youth. I never met a young man in a public park on Sunday morning wheeling his first baby in a perambulator without feeling an ache of reverence.

–James Douglas

He that hath wife and children hath given hostages to fortune; for they are impediments to great enterprises, either of virtue or mischief.

—Francis Bacon

Fatherhood wreaks havoc with our car mythology. The dreams on which we came of age — swanky images of Italian sports cars, reconditioned 'Vettes — are replaced by station-wagon realities. Once he's a father, the same guy who imagined himself hairpinning through the Alps in a Lamborghini is driving a minivan very carefully.

—Hugh O'Neill

[L]ook at my dad. He was twenty when he started having a family, and he was always the coolest dad. He did everything for his kids, and he never made us feel like he was pressured. I know that it must be a great feeling to be a guy like that.

—Adam Sandler

Happy is the child whose father acquits himself with credit in the presence of his friends.

—Robert Lynd

⚜

Boys and girls need chances to be around their father, to be enjoyed by him and if possible to do things with him. Better to play fifteen minutes enjoyably and then say, "Now I'm going to read my paper" than to spend all day at the zoo crossly.

—Dr. Benjamin Spock
Dr. Spock's Baby and Child Care

men derive more genuine undutiful amusement and companionship from youngsters than do women.

—Hilda Cole Espy

I have these slumber parties with my father where we stay up all night trading beauty tips. He knows all about the good creams and masks.

—Liv Tyler on her father Steven Tyler

To show a child what has once delighted you, to find the child's delight added to your own, so that there is now a double delight seen in the glow of trust and affection, this is happiness.

—J. B. Priestley

YOU CAN DO ANYTHING WITH CHILDREN IF YOU ONLY PLAY WITH THEM.

—PRINCE OTTO VON BISMARCK (ATTR.)

What was it, this being "a good father"? To love one's sons and daughters was not enough; to carry in one's bone and blood a pride in them, a longing for their growth and development—this was not enough. One had to be a ready companion to games and jokes and outings, to earn from the world this accolade. The devil with it.

—Laura Z. Hobson

My son is seven years old. I am fifty-four. It has taken me a great many years to reach that age. I am more respected in the community, I am stronger, I am more intelligent, and I think I am better than he is. I don't want to be a pal. I want to be a father.

—Clifton Fadiman

[P]robably even more useful to a four-year-old than Batman and the Ninja Turtles is a father who is right there when he's needed to punch out a whale or banish brontosaurs from the hall closet.

—S. Adams Sullivan

I COULD NOT POINT TO ANY NEED IN CHILDHOOD AS STRONG AS THAT FOR A FATHER'S PROTECTION.

—SIGMUND FREUD

My father would walk through flaming barbed wire for you. I mean, for his family, for anybody. When you know your family is there like that it's **a great source of strength and reassurance.**

—Michael J. Fox

When I was a kid, I used to imagine animals running under my bed. I told my dad, and he solved the problem quickly. **He cut the legs off my bed.**

—Lou Brock

Safe, for a child, is his father's hand, holding him tight.

—Marion C. Garretty

A man wants to protect his son, wants to teach him the things he, the father, has learned or thinks he has learned. But it's exactly that which a child resents. He wants to know, but he wants to know on his own—and the longer the paternal influence lasts, the harder it is to break down and the more two individuals who should have much in common are pushed apart.

—William Carlos Williams

We can't form our children on our own concepts; we must take them and love them as God gives them to us. **Raise them the best we can, and leave them free to develop.**

—Johann Wolfgang von Goethe

Parentage is a very important profession; but no test of fitness for it is ever imposed in the interest of the children.

—George Bernard Shaw

Here, Dad. I'd like you to sign this form and have it notarized:

"I, the undersigned Dad, attest that I have never parented before, and insofar as I have no experience in the job, I am liable for my mistakes and agree to pay for any counseling in perpetuity Calvin may require as a result of my parental ineptitude."

I don't see how you're allowed to have a kid without signing one of those!

—Bill Watterson
"Calvin and Hobbes"

All Father's experience as a parent was obtained at my hands. He was a man who had many impossible hopes for his children, and it was only as he tried these on me that he slowly became disillusioned.

—Clarence Day

Parenting means feeling, but it also means doing all sorts of boring tasks, taking children to school, buying them jackets, attending band concerts, dealing with curfews, **setting rules of behavior. . . .**

—Robert Bly
Iron John

MY FATHER WOULD NOT GET US A TV; HE WOULDN'T ALLOW A TV IN THE HOUSE.

—JANIS JOPLIN

I don't know why men are so fascinated with television, and I think it has something to do with—if I may judge from my own father, who used to sit and stare at the TV while my mother was speaking to him—I think that's a man's way of tuning out.

—Garry Shandling

My father hated radio and he could not wait for television to be invented so that he could hate that too.

—Peter De Vries

What a dreadful thing it must be to have a dull father. . . .

–Mary Mapes Dodge

If the statistics are true, by the time the average American youngster is six, he will spend more time watching television than he will spend talking to his father in his lifetime.

—Dr. James Dobson
Children at Risk

The mother may do 90 percent of the disciplining, but the father still must have a full-time acceptance of all the children. He must never say, "Get these kids out of here; I'm trying to watch TV."

—BILL COSBY

You can hit my father over the head with a chair and he won't wake up, but my mother, all you have to do to my mother is cough somewhere in Siberia and she'll hear you.

—J. D. Salinger
The Catcher in the Rye

MR. MOM

Approximately 143,000 American men are stay-at-home dads, according to the U.S. Census Bureau. The Bureau defines them as married fathers with children under age 15 who have remained outside the workforce for more than one year primarily to provide child care while their wives work outside the home.

I wasn't allowed to go to movies when I was a kid; my father was a minister. *101 Dalmatians* and *King of Kings*, that was the extent of it.

—Denzel Washington

A stodgy parent is no fun at all. What a child wants and deserves is **a parent who is sparky**.

—Roald Dahl

I miss my Dad. My Dad loved cheesy monster movies, so we'd have Godzilla movie marathons. Those are some of my favorite memories, laughing at how the monster outfits were so bad, like black garbage bags for heads.

—Ahmet Zappa

As far as rearing children goes, the basic idea I try to keep in mind is that a child is a person. Just because they happen to be a little shorter than you doesn't mean they are dumber than you.

—Frank Zappa

I'm a fun father, but not a good father. The hard decisions always went to my wife.

–John Lithgow

When one [of your children] comes to you and says, "Dad, can I go explore the Upper Nile?" your answer must be, "Go ask your mother."

—Bill Cosby
Fatherhood

Fathers are not male mothers. Fathers will find that as they spend time with their children, they'll develop their own unique ways of loving and parenting their children.

—MICHAEL HOROWITZ, PhD

In a mode that can be quite different from that of a mother, a father conveys to his children . . . the often reasonable, sometimes harsh, always inescapable, rules, expectations, and inevitabilities of life.

— Mark O'Connell, PhD

When a father is indulgent, he is more indulgent than a mother. Little ones treat their mother as the authority of rule, and their father as the authority of dispensation.

—Frederick W. Faber
Bethlehem

How can one say no to a child? How can one be anything but a slave to one's own flesh and blood?

—Henry Miller

I have found that the best way to give advice to your children is to find out what they want, and then advise them to do it.

—Harry S Truman

IT IS a WISE FaTHer THaT KNOWS HIS OWN CHILD.

—William Shakespeare

In order not to influence a child, one must be careful not to be that child's parent or grandparent.

–Don Marquis

IF I'M MORE OF aN INFLUence TO YOUR SON as a rapper THaN YOU are as a FaTHer . . . YOU GOT TO LOOK aT YOURSELF as a PareNT.

—Ice Cube

They still come to their old dad with their problems. I like that. I like listening and then with the wisdom of age giving them my heartfelt advice. I even like the fact that they then go out and do exactly what they wanted to do anyway—that's the way it should be with parents and kids.

—Perry Como

DON'T WORRY THAT CHILDREN NEVER LISTEN TO YOU; WORRY THAT THEY ARE ALWAYS WATCHING YOU.

—ROBERT FULGHUM

To bring up a child in the way he should go, travel that way yourself once in a while.

—Josh Billings

In all candor, I cannot say that I know for sure just how seriously my own children listen to me, but, God bless them, they at least pretend they do.

—Adlai E. Stevenson

The quickest way for a parent to get a child's attention is to sit down and look comfortable.

—Lane Olinghouse

Any kid will run any errand for you if you ask at bedtime.

—Red Skelton

Raising children is part joy
and part guerrilla warfare.

—**Ed Asner**

When dealing with a two-year-old in the midst of a tantrum, fathers need to be particularly **watchful about the tendency to need to feel victorious.**

—Dr. Kyle Pruett

I do not love him because he is good,
but because he is my little child.
—Rabindranath Tagore

How many children do you have?
No children.
No children—what do you do for aggravation?

> —YIDDISH PROVERB

Selective ignorance, a cornerstone of child rearing. You don't put kids under surveillance: it might frighten you. Parents should sit tall in the saddle and look upon their troops with a noble and benevolent and extremely nearsighted gaze.

> —Garrison Keillor

Men are generally more careful of the breed of their horses and dogs than of their children.

—William Penn

WHEN CHILDREN ARE DOING NOTHING, THEY ARE DOING MISCHIEF.

—HENRY FIELDING

Never teach your child to be cunning for you may be certain that you will be one of the first victims of his shrewdness.

—Josh Billings

You can learn many things from children. How much patience you have, for instance.

—Franklin P. Adams

When I was a kid, I said to my father one afternoon, "Daddy, will you take me to the zoo?" He answered, **"If the zoo wants you, let them come and get you."**

—Jerry Lewis

I had never traveled before. When we were kids, my father would be, like, "What's the point? We're happy here. Let's just stay at home."

—Kyle MacLachlan

The memories of my family outings are still a source of strength to me. I remember we'd all pile into the car—I forget what kind it was—and drive and drive. I'm not sure where we'd go, but I think there were some trees there. . . . I remember a bigger, older guy we called "Dad." We'd eat some stuff, or not, and then I think we went home. I guess some things never leave you.

—Jack Handey
Deep Thoughts

Parents who expect gratitude from their children (there are even some who insist on it) are like usurers who gladly risk their capital if only they receive interest.

—Franz Kafka

HAPPY IS THE FATHER WHOSE CHILD FINDS HIS ATTEMPTS TO AMUSE IT AMUSING.

—ROBERT LYND

It is a wise child that knows its own father.

—Robert Greene, 1589

IT IS A WISE CHILD THAT KNOWS HIS OWN FATHER, AND AN UNUSUAL ONE THAT UNRESERVEDLY APPROVES OF HIM.

—MARK TWAIN

Children begin by loving their parents.
After a while, they judge them. Rarely, if
ever, do they forgive them.

—Oscar Wilde

Parents were invented to make children
happy by giving them something to ignore.

—Ogden Nash

What is it that makes somebody a good
parent? It has to do with constancy. It has
to do with love. . . . I don't know where it's
written that a woman has a corner on that
market, that a man has any less of those
emotions than a woman does.

—Ted Kramer, played by Dustin Hoffman
in the movie *Kramer vs Kramer*

But as a society we are still waiting for the **"new fatherhood"** to happen. The era when most fathers and most mothers will have equal parenting roles definitely isn't here yet.

—S. Adams Sullivan

Consistent dads . . . **help us feel secure in the world and allow us to trust others.**

—Stephan B. Poulter, PhD

Just because Mom always fixes every little bump with a hug and a kiss doesn't mean that Dad can't make things better with words of **"shake it off, little guy."**

—Julie Bort, Aviva Pflock, and Devra Renner
Mommy Guilt

The words that a father speaks to his children in the privacy of home are not heard by the world, but, as in whispering-galleries, they are clearly heard at the end and by posterity.

—Jean Paul Richter

A child enters your home and makes so much noise for twenty years that you can hardly stand it: then departs leaving the house so silent that you think you will go mad.

—John Andrew Holmes

You know when your children are growing up when they stop asking you where they came from and **refuse to tell you where they are going.**

—P. J. O'Rourke

There are only two lasting legacies we can hope to give our children. **One of these is roots; the other, wings.**

—Hodding Carter

Frontier Justice:
Dad the Disciplinarian

Just wait until your father gets home.

—mothers everywhere

Father was the head of the house in true Germanic tradition, and not a one of us would have dared to cross him.

—Lawrence Welk

Whenever my dad got mad at me or my brother, he would never actually hit us. But he did have one of the great belt movements. He'd say, "Do I have to go for the belt?" Then he'd wiggle his waistband around a little—kind of fatherly Morse code for impending doom. Usually this was enough to have me say, "Oh, no, Pop! Everything's all right!"

—Jay Leno

My father's bark was always more to be feared than his bite. He would threaten loudly, but punish mildly or not at all.

—John Burroughs

"Yes, they are good boys," I once heard a kind father say. "I talk to them very much, but do not like to beat my children—the world will beat them."

—Elihu Burritt

THAT'LL TEACH YOU

A 1646 Massachusetts law provided that a child over the age of sixteen "who shall curse or smite their natural father or mother ... shall be put to death."

As nothing can joy the heart of a father more than the obedience of a loving child, so can there be nothing more grievous than a stubborn spirit of an ungracious son. . . .

—Nicholas Breton

♕

FaTHer . . . LOOKeD UPOn CHILDren as raw maTerIaL THaT a FaTHer SHOULD MOLD.

—Clarence Day
Life with Father

My dad did not like me enough to hit. My dad thought he was disciplining. . . . He always thought he was doing the right thing, and he did not like me enough to do the right thing by me. Which would have been to whip me—literally—into shape.

— Danny Bonaduce

He that spareth his rod hateth his son; but he that loveth him chasteneth him betimes.

–Proverbs 13:24

Whipping will work but an imperfect cure ... frequent beating is therefore to be avoided.

– Michel de Montaigne

My father and I were always on the most distant terms when I was a boy—a sort of armed neutrality, so to speak. At irregular intervals this neutrality was broken, and suffering ensued; but I will be candid enough to say that the breaking and the suffering were always divided with strict impartiality between us—which is to say, my father did the breaking and I did the suffering.

—Mark Twain

Father, chancing to chastise
His indignant daughter Sue,
Said: "I hope you realize
That this hurts me more than you."

Susan straightaway ceased to roar;
"If that's really true," said she,
"I can stand a good deal more;
Pray go on, and don't mind me."

—Harry Graham
Ruthless Rhymes, 1899

I am convinced that if parents knew the
benefits of not hitting their children and
the risk they were exposing them to when
they spank, millions would stop.

—Murray Straus

I spanked my children . . . not because I had given it a lot of thought or believed that children needed to be spanked or I had reached the end of my rope, but simply because I felt like it.

—J. Rosemond

Many a father spanks his child for things his father should have spanked out of him.

—Don Marquis

Should one spank? I believe ... that the answer to this question is a resounding "Maybe, but, very possibly, maybe not."

—Mark O'Connell, PhD

Don't be a lion in your own house.

—Czech Proverb

"I brought you into this world," my father would say, "and I can take you out. It don't make no difference to me. I'll just make another one like you."

—Bill Cosby

Have a Baby, My Wife Just Had a Cigar

The custom of a father handing out cigars to announce the birth of a child originated among Native Americans of the Pacific Northwest as a variant of the potlatch, where a man gives away his wealth to celebrate a birth or wedding.

Even very young children need to be informed about dying. Explain the concept of death very carefully to your child. This will make threatening him with it **much more effective.**

—P. J. O'Rourke

My father believed in frontier justice. He'd say, "I don't know who broke the clock in the front hall, so you're all going to be punished." It seemed unfair at the time, but now that it has become the basis of our foreign policy, I'm starting to think my father was on to something.

—Conan O'Brien

MY FATHER WAS AFRAID OF HIS FATHER, I WAS AFRAID OF MY FATHER, AND I DON'T SEE WHY MY CHILDREN SHOULDN'T BE AFRAID OF ME.

—LORD MOUNTBATTEN

Love and fear. Everything the father of the family says must inspire one or the other.

—Joseph Joubert

My father was very loving but very severe; his severity made him the more endearing. In my relations with him I was like the people who live at the foot of a volcano. . . . Each morning and evening is displayed a new and charming aspect of the mountain, but all at once it will send up huge columns of fire and emit voluminous heavy stones from its quiet cone, the sight of which can never be erased from one's memory.

—Kazuo Koizumi

The fathers have eaten a sour grape, and the children's teeth are set on edge.

—Jeremiah 31:29

WE'RE NOT LOST: *Dad's Favorite Phrases*

· Don't ask me—ask your mother.

· You live under my roof, you live by my rules.

· Don't use that tone with me!

· You're not leaving the house dressed like that, young lady!

· If I've told you once, I've told you a thousand times.

· I'm not asleep. I'm just resting my eyes.

· You're going to eat it, and you're going to like it.

· Nobody said life was fair.

· For the last time, we're not lost.

· That's it. Get out of the car. Now!

· I don't need directions. I know where it is.

· You really ought to visit more often. Your mother worries.

· This is just between you and me—don't tell your mother.

MY MOTHER PROTECTED ME FROM THE WORLD AND MY FATHER THREATENED ME WITH IT.

—QUENTIN CRISP

Fathers, provoke not your children to anger, lest they be discouraged.

—Colossians 3:21

A torn jacket is soon mended, **but hard words bruise the heart of a child.**

—Henry Wadsworth Longfellow

Any father whose son raises his hand against him is guilty of having produced a son who raised his hand against him.

—Charles Peguy

Never raise your hand to your kids.
It leaves your groin unprotected.

—Red Buttons

If you must hold yourself up to your children as an object lesson, hold yourself up as a warning and not as an example.

—George Bernard Shaw

I have sometimes thought that a thoroughly judicious father is one of the rarest creatures to be met with.

—Sir Arthur Helps

Nothing Dearer: Fathers and Daughters

The lucky man has a daughter as his first child.

—Spanish proverb

Seeing Natasha on that ultrasound screen and knowing that she was going to be a little girl was one of the greatest moments in my life.

—Quinton Skinner

I love my family very much. And here's the part where I become the cliché father: I have never in my life thought it was possible to feel such deep love, such an incredible connection to this amazing little human being. She's an angel.

—Johnny Depp on his daughter

I ONLY HaVe TWO rULes FOr mY newLY BOrn DaUGHTer: sHe WILL Dress weLL anD never Have sex.

—JOHN MALKOVICH

The father of a daughter is nothing but a high-class hostage. A father turns a stony face to his sons, berates them, shakes his antlers, paws the ground, snorts, runs them off into the underbrush, but when his daughter puts her arm over his shoulder and says, "Daddy, I need to ask you something," he is a pat of butter in a hot frying pan.

—Garrison Keillor

When Charles first saw our child Mary, he said all the proper things for a new father. He looked upon the poor little red thing and blurted, "She's more beautiful than the Brooklyn Bridge."

—Helen Hayes

I think a girl who doesn't have a good relationship with her father has such a disadvantage in life, because fathers can give you such esteem, such confidence in yourself. As you make your way in the world, it's good to know that, from a male standpoint, there's someone who cares about you and thinks you are the greatest, most beautiful thing.

—Gayle King

I'm not jealous of Margot, never have been. I don't envy her good looks or her beauty. It is only that I long for Daddy's real love: not only as his child, but for me—**Anne, myself.**

—Anne Frank

Certain is it that there is no kind of affection so purely angelic as of a father to a daughter. In love to our wives there is desire; to our sons, ambition; but to our daughters there is something which there are no words to express.

—Joseph Addison

There's something like a line of gold thread running through a man's words when he talks to his daughter, and gradually over the years it gets to be long enough for you to pick up in your hands and weave into a cloth that feels like love itself.

—John Gregory Brown

I find myself enjoying a deeper love than I ever imagined was possible in the form of my daughter and certainly in the union with my wife. It makes everything else, including my work, which is one of the things I'm most passionate about, pale by comparison.

—Benjamin Bratt

I never had a father, and that was always a big issue in my life.

—Nastassja Kinski

I owe just about everything to my father [and] it's passionately interesting for me that the things that I learned in a small town, in a very modest home, are just the things that **I believe have won the election.**

—Former British Prime Minister Margaret Thatcher

My dear father; my dear friend; the best and wisest man I ever knew, who taught me many lessons and showed me many things as we went together along the country byways.

—Sarah Orne Jewett

My father praised me and comforted me.
That made me so happy that nothing else mattered.
—Anna Freud

I have always had the feeling
I could do anything and my dad told me
I could. I was in college before I found
out he might be wrong.
—ANN RICHARDS

It's like the father has a special power
of pronouncing the daughter worthy and accept-
able. Women have mom more as a friend, but
they depend on fathers more in terms of who
they are, in terms of identity.
—Terry Hargrave

My father never put any pressure on me to be anybody but myself, so I feel that I've done him proud certainly. He thinks I'm a good kid and that I've done well for myself and he's very proud of me.

—Cameron Diaz

It was not always easy because I was always an individual and found it difficult to be one of a group. One person who was very supportive was my father. My mother was great but my father really recognized my individuality and supported me in that.

–Sharon Stone

WITH a SONG IN HIS HEART

The father-daughter wedding dance is an enduring tradition, and there's a song for almost every taste. Among the most popular are "Daddy's Little Girl" by the Mills Brothers, "I Loved Her First" by Heartland, and the duet of Nat King Cole and Natalie Cole singing "Unforgettable."

All my children have spoken for themselves since they first learned to speak, and not always with my advance approval, and I expect that to continue in the future.

–Gerald R. Ford

Dad always listened to me before making a judgment or decision. And he would help me think through things before I had to make an important decision.

—Susan Ford Bales on her
father Gerald R. Ford

Good fathers not only give daughters love and affection, they also teach them to be daring. Fathers teach daughters that they can succeed, that they have what it takes to fulfill their dreams in a world in which what they do and where they go in their future is up to them.

—Dr. Joyce Brothers

MY MOTHER GAVE ME MY DRIVE, BUT MY FATHER GAVE ME MY DREAMS.

—Liza Minnelli

I was brought up on art. My father thought I had a great hand at art and sent me to art school. But he did not want me to become a photographer.

—IMOGEN CUNNINGHAM

My dad wasn't thrilled at my wanting to act. He even offered to pay for a computer course if I'd change my mind.

–Marcia Gay Harden

To depend upon a profession is a less odious form of slavery than to **depend upon a father.**

—Virginia Woolf

All right, I'll give you fifty dollars to help pay your expenses for a couple of weeks, until you recover from this madness, but that's the last penny you'll get from me until you do something respectable.

—Thomas Hepburn to his daughter
   Katharine on her acting career

When you give me this award, you honor my father, Paul Sorvino, who has taught me everything there is to know about acting.

—Mira Sorvino, accepting 1996
Best Supporting Actress Academy Award

Things with my dad were pretty good until
I won an Academy Award. He was really
loving to me until I got more attention than
he did. Then he hated me.

—Tatum O'Neal

The bitterest "fact" of all is, that I had
believed Papa to have loved me more
than he obviously does: but I never regret
knowledge—I mean I would never unknow
anything—even were it the taste of apples
by the Dead Sea—and this must be
accepted like the rest.

—Elizabeth Barrett Browning

I never could dance around you, my father. No one ever danced around you. As soon as I left you, my father, the whole world swung into a symphony.

—Anaïs Nin

A father's remoteness may severely damage the daughter's ability to participate good-heartedly in later relationships with men.

—Robert Bly

A GUY
LIKE DAD

A study conducted at the University of Chicago found that men influence their daughters' choice of mates more than they could imagine. Women tend to prefer the smell of a mate whose genetic makeup is similar to genes they have inherited from their fathers but not their mothers.

I spent the first twenty years of my life waiting for two men I was reasonably certain would never come back—my daddy and Jesus Christ. I don't wait for them anymore. My dad, anyway. And at least with Jesus I didn't spend all that time thinking he was gone because of something I did.

—BRETT BUTLER

MY FATHER WAS OFTEN ANGRY WHEN I WAS MOST LIKE HIM.

—LILLIAN HELLMAN

I passed through a terrible scourging when last at my father's. I cannot tell you how deep the iron entered my soul. I never felt more deeply the degradation of my sex. To think that all in me of which my father would have felt a proper pride had I been a man, is deeply mortifying to him because I am a woman.

—Elizabeth Cady Stanton

I'm female, thank God, because if I was male this really would be difficult. And, of course, I don't attempt to sound like my father—I do my own thing.

—Lisa Marie Presley

My father was a statesman. I'm a political woman. My father was a saint. I'm not.

—Indira Gandhi

My aunts and grandmother would tell my sister, brother, our cousins, and me stories of their childhood, and my father's. We loved to listen to any tales that revealed him as a less than perfect child.

—Cokie Roberts

In matching wits with Dad, my brother and
I did not have to agree with him, but we had to be
prepared to defend our views. After coming to
Washington, I used to phone home weekly, and
Dad and I continued a discussion that had its start
at the dinner table years ago. Dad never hesitated
to let me know when he disagreed . . . and I still
needed to be prepared to defend my votes.

—former U.S. Senator Nancy Landon Kassebaum
on her father Alf Landon

My father was very strong. I don't
agree with a lot of the ways he brought me up.
I don't agree with a lot of his values, but he did
have a lot of integrity, and if he told us not to do
something, he didn't do it either.

— Madonna Ciccone

It isn't that I'm a weak father, it's just that she's a strong daughter.

—Henry Fonda on his daughter Jane

I can run the country or control Alice. I can't do both.

—President Theodore Roosevelt on his daughter

I have done everything I can to make sure my daughter knows her father because you form your own identity by rebelling against your parents—but first you have to know them.

—Greta Scacchi

I love my dad, although I'm definitely critical of him some-times, like when his pants are too tight. But I love him so much, and I try to be really supportive of him.

—Liv Tyler

Every American daughter is
an authority on fashion, and one of the things she knows is that her father dresses like somebody in the Mummers Parade.
—Bill Cosby

My dad was so open creatively that I was off in search of black turtleneck bathing suits with long sleeves.

—MOON UNIT ZAPPA

It is admirable for a man to take his son fishing, but there is a special place in heaven for the father who takes his daughter shopping.

—John Sinor

My dad was very fun and very adventurous, and from a formative age I learned to value men who would do things on a whim.

–Rachel Hunter

My dad took me to all the best rock and punk shows when I was growing up and music has always been a part of my life. So I'm very interested in the music scene and I suppose that's why I've ended up going out with musicians.

—Winona Ryder

Watching your daughter being collected by her date feels like handing over a million dollar Stradivarius to a gorilla.

—Jim Bishop

The thing to remember about fathers is, they're men. A girl has to keep it in mind: They are dragon-seekers, bent on improbable rescues. Scratch any father, you find someone chock-full of qualms and romantic terrors, believing change is a threat—like your first shoes with heels on, like your first bicycle it took such months to get.

—Phyllis McGinley

MANY a man wishes he were strong enough to tear a telephone book in half—especially if he has a teenage daughter.

—Guy Lombardo

Any astronomer can predict with absolute accuracy just where every star in the universe will be at 11:30 tonight. He can make no such prediction about his teenage daughter.

—James T. Adams

Dating? People think I'll be one of those dads with the shotgun at the gate, but I haven't even thought about that yet.

—Sean "Diddy" Combs on his twin daughters

My father has taught me **all the tricks** of the boys at an early age, which has made me very careful.

—Kim Wilde

It is no new observation, I believe, that a lover in most cases has no rival so much to be feared as the father.

—Charles Lamb

I am not ashamed to say that no man I ever met was my father's equal, and I never loved any other man as much.

—Hedy Lamarr

I always worry about what my male will be like, because I want him to be as wonderful as my father, but I don't think it's possible. Popsy is hard-working, good looking, fun-loving, faith-ful, and he likes music. Besides he's smart. If I expect all that I will end up an old maid. (Maybe I oudda just settle for good looks.)

—Joan Baez in teenage journal

My father set the bar very high for the man who was going to be in my life. He was very much a gentleman, always taking my mother's arm and my arm whenever we crossed the street. I knew that was how a man should be.

—Susan Lucci

Daddy was real gentle with kids. That's why I expected so much out of marriage, figuring that all men should be steady and pleasant.

—Loretta Lynn

I know that I will never find my father in any other man who comes into my life, because it is a void in my life that can only be filled by him.

—Halle Berry

[My father] is a nice guy. He would come home every night for dinner at six. He would send me to the college I wanted to go to. He was always consistent and reliable and made me expect men to be that way. Because of the way he was, I married a decent man.

—Myrna Blyth

You worry about [your daughter] going out with the wrong kind of guys. . . . Then she gets a little older and you quit worrying about her meeting the wrong guy and you worry about her meeting the right guy and that's the biggest fear of all because then you'd lose her.

—George Banks as played by Steve Martin
in *Father of the Bride*

I was so proud of you and thrilled at having you so close to me on our long walk in Westminster Abbey, but when I handed your hand to the archbishop, I felt that I had lost something very precious.

—King George VI to his daughter Princess Elizabeth
on her marriage to Prince Philip

One of life's greatest mysteries is how the boy who wasn't good enough to marry your daughter can be the father of the smartest grandchild in the world.

—Proverb

Tell me, my daughters,
Since now we will divest us Both of rule,
Interest of territory, cares of State,
Which of you shall we say doth love us most?

—King Lear to his three daughters in
King Lear by William Shakespeare

TO A FATHER GROWING OLD NOTHING IS DEARER THAN A DAUGHTER.

—EURIPIDES

You mustn't get aggravated when your old dad calls you his baby, because he always will think of you as just that—no matter how old or big you may get.

—Harry S Truman to his daughter Margaret

A father is always making his baby into a little woman. And when she is a woman, he turns her back again.

–Enid Bagnold

OLD AS SHE WAS, SHE STILL MISSED HER DADDY SOMETIMES.

—Gloria Naylor

My father died many years ago, and yet when something special happens to me, I talk to him secretly not really knowing whether he hears, but it makes me feel better to half believe it.

—Natasha Josefowitz

WHEN MY DAD DIED a LOT OF SONGS CAME, AND THEY'RE STILL COMING.

—Rosanne Cash

It doesn't matter who my father was; **it matters who I remember he was.**

—Anne Sexton

A Nervous Breakdown into Innings: Dads and Sports

Baseball is the president tossing out the first ball of the season and a scrubby schoolboy playing catch with his dad on a Mississippi farm.

—Ernie Harwell

My dad was . . . just infatuated with baseball. He was the one that basically taught me how to play the game. He gave a lot of his time working out with me, practicing, and taking me to a lot of different games. It was hard work between both of us.

—Rafael Palmeiro

Baseball is fathers and sons PLAYING CATCH, LAZY AND MURDEROUS, WILD AND CONTROLLED, THE PROFOUND ARCHAIC SONG OF BIRTH, GROWTH, AGE, AND DEATH.

—DONALD HALL

My father used to play with my brother and me in the yard. Mother would come out and say, "You're tearing up the grass." "We're not raising grass," Dad would reply. **"We're raising boys."**

—Harmon Killebrew

My brother Tony was the best ballplayer in the family. My dad wouldn't let him go. And I always kidded my dad, I said, "See that, Pops? You let all your sons go, you'd have been a millionaire." He said, "Blame your mother."

—Yogi Berra

My dad taught me to switch-hit.

He and my grandfather, who was left-handed, pitched to me every day after school in the backyard. I batted lefty against my dad and righty against my granddad.

—Mickey Mantle

Great Sports

Dick Hoyt and his quadriplegic son Rick have competed in more than 900 racing events since first competing in the Boston Marathon in 1981. When competing as runners, Dick pushes Rick in a wheelchair. When they swim, Dick tows Rick in a small boat. When they cycle, Rick sits on a seat attached to the front of Dick's bike.

My dad had been a shortstop when he was in college, and you know, **when you're a kid, you want to be just like your dad.**

—Derek Jeter

My father said to me, "You're not going into a cotton field, that's number one." That means picking cotton down there, putting it in a sack, carrying it on your shoulder. "You're not going to do that. You're going to play baseball."

–Willie Mays

When I was six years old, my father taught me that wonderful and mysterious art of keeping score, so that when he went to work during the day, I could stay home and record the history of that day's Brooklyn Dodger game, play by play, inning by inning. And at night when he would come home, and you're only six years old, and he tells you, **"You're doing great as a miniature historian."**

—**Doris Kearns Goodwin**

For the parents of a Little Leaguer, a baseball game is simply a nervous breakdown into innings.

–Earl Wilson

I THINK LITTLE LEAGUE IS WONDERFUL. IT KEEPS THE KIDS OUT OF THE HOUSE.

—Yogi Berra

I was a very good baseball and football player, but my father always told me I was much more interested in how I looked playing baseball or football than in actually playing. There's great truth in that.

—John Malkovich

I am delighted to have you play football. I believe in rough, manly sports. But I do not believe in them if they degenerate into the sole end of anyone's existence.

—THEODORE ROOSEVELT TO HIS SON
THEODORE ROOSEVELT, JR.

As I get older, kids are definitely something I want to do. I remember my dad coming home at night after work and having a beer. And then we'd run patterns for his football passes. One day I want to do that.

—Luke Wilson

John Elway is a great football player. He used to be my son. Now I'm his father.

–Jack Elway

My father was a great influence. He was a real jock. He was an all-American football player, a quarterback at West Point, part of the great winning team of 1917. He was captain of the team. I was the mascot. They lost the game to Navy. Nobody's perfect. But his character was a great stimulus to me.

—Gore Vidal

YOU KNOW MY DAD PUSHED ME TO BELIEVE THAT I WAS GOING TO BE THE BEST. I JUST NEVER THOUGHT OF LIFE WITHOUT TENNIS.

—ANDRE AGASSI

I was so happy. I look back on that time with such happiness. It was never about being a great tennis player or being ambitious. Dad wasn't like that. He was ambitious, but it was just about having fun.

—MONICA SELES

A MAN'S WORLD

The father's genetic contribution to conceiving a baby determines the child's gender—which may explain why among humans, about 105 boys are born for every 100 girls.

It wasn't like I was self-motivated. My dad started me. It was his dream before it was mine.

—Venus Williams

I have avoided tennis for a long time because there was a great deal of pressure for me to play tennis. My dad played tennis.

–Brooke Shields

👑

Don't force your kids into sports. I never was. To this day, my dad has never asked me to go play golf. I ask him. It's the child's desire to play that matters, not the parent's desire to have the child play. Fun. **Keep it fun.**

—Tiger Woods

When I was three . . . my father put my hands in his and placed them around the shaft of a cut-down women's golf club. He showed me the classic overlap, or Vardon grip—the proper grip for a good golf swing he said—and told me to hit the golf ball. . . . "Hit it hard boy. Go find it and hit it again."

—Arnold Palmer

I want to get beyond the courtesy stage. My father and I have a ritual: Whenever I go home, we play golf together.

–Kyle MacLachlan

The place of the father in the modern suburban family is a very small one, particularly if he plays golf.

—Bertrand Russell

I went and took golf lessons so dad would let me play with him. I was just terrible . . . but I was able to have a wonderful time just walking around with dad.

—David Hyde Pierce

Somewhere in my wildest childhood I must have done something right. Being able to make a boyhood dream come true is one thing, but to have a kid come along and thrill his dad like Brett Hull has thrilled me over his career is too much for one guy to handle.

—Bobby Hull

MY DAD WAS MY BIGGEST SUPPORTER. HE NEVER PUT PRESSURE ON ME.

—BOBBY ORR

My dad was very successful running midgets in Texas. Then, his two drivers ran into some bad luck. People started saying that Daddy had lost his touch. That it was the cars and not the drivers. I wanted to race just to prove all those people wrong.

—A. J. Foyt

DAD TAUGHT ME EVERY-THING I KNOW. UNFORTU-NATELY, HE DIDN'T TEACH ME EVERYTHING HE KNOWS.

—AL UNSER

To be a great ballplayer or any sort of great athlete, you need more than just physical ability. You also need keen mental awareness and a deep emotional involvement. These are the same three key components of great fathering.

—Jack Petrash

Our Similarities Are Different:
Fathers and Sons

'TIS a HaPPY THING TO BE THE FATHER UNTO many sons.

—WILLIAM SHAKESPEARE, *King Henry VI*

All fathers entertain the pious wish of seeing their own lacks realized in their sons. It is quite as though one could live for a second time and put in full use all the experience of one's first career. . . .

—JOHANN WOLFGANG VON GOETHE

Dad made his first flight in 1918 and jumped in a self-packed parachute in 1920. He trained fighter pilots in World War II. . . . Dad was the first American businessman to fly his own plane abroad. And it was in this very plane, a Lockheed Vega, that I experienced my first ride into the wild blue yonder, with Dad at the throttle.

—Dr. Buzz Aldrin, one of first two
men to walk on the moon

It is a great moment in life when a father sees a son grow taller than he or reach farther.
—Richard L. Evans

My father taught me to finish anything I started. And I think that carries throughout your adult life. Most people's personalities and moralities are formed when they are rather young, and that characteristic will **carry out throughout their lifetime.**

—General Chuck Yeager

You don't raise heroes, you raise sons. And if you treat them like sons, they'll turn out to be heroes, even if it's just in your own eyes.

—Walter M. Schirra, Sr.

I was born February 6, 1911, in a flat above the local bank in Tampico, Illinois. According to family legend, when my father ran up the stairs and looked at his newborn son, he quipped: "He looks like a fat little Dutchman. But who knows, he might grow up to be president some day."

—Ronald Reagan

THE FATHER IN PRAISING HIS SON EXTOLS HIMSELF.

—CHINESE PROVERB

It is funny the two things most men are proudest of is the thing that any man can do and doing does in the same way, that is being drunk and being the father of their son.

—GERTRUDE STEIN

The search for a father is as crucial as the need for a son, and the search of each for the other—through all the days of one's life—exempts no one. Happy is the man who finds both.

—MAX LERNER

**I know what a father means because
I didn't have a father.**

—Larry King

**No adult in my family would ever tell me
anything about who my father was** . . . and
it probably was a gift to my imagination that my
mother wouldn't talk about him, because . . . you
begin to invent who your father might have been,
and this becomes a secret, a private obsession,
which I would say is an apt description of writing
novels and screenplays, **of making things up
in lieu of knowing the real answer.**

—John Irving

My father left me with the feeling that I had to live for two people, and that if I did it well enough, somehow I could make up for the life he should have had.

—Bill Clinton on his father,
who died before he was born

Children make fictions of their fathers, reinventing them according to their childish needs. The reality of a father is a weight few sons can bear.

—Salman Rushdie

I had not known my father very well. We had got on badly, partly because we shared, in our different fashions, the vice of stubborn pride. When he was dead I realized that I had hardly ever spoken to him. When he had been dead a long time I began to wish I had.

—James Baldwin

LIKE FATHER LIKE SON.
—Thomas Draxe, 1616

For rarely are sons similar to their fathers: most are worse, and a few are better than their fathers.

—Homer

Greatness of name in the father oft-times overwhelms the son; they stand too near one another. The shadow kills the growth: so much, that we see the grandchild come more and oftener to be heir of the first.

—Ben Jonson

I always wanted to be better than my father as a singer.

— Enrique Iglesias on his father Julio Iglesias

YOU CAN'T COMPARE ME TO MY FATHER. OUR SIMILARITIES ARE DIFFERENT.

—DALE BERRA, SON OF YOGI BERRA

I grew up to have my father's looks—my father's speech patterns—my father's posture—my father's walk—my father's opinions and my mother's contempt for my father.

—JULES FEIFFER

What was silent in the father speaks in the son, and often I found in the son the unveiled secret of the father.

—Friedrich Wilhelm Nietzsche

A boy, by the age of three years, senses that his destiny is to be a man, so he watches his father particularly—his interests, manner, speech, pleasures, his attitude toward work.

—Dr. Benjamin Spock and Michael B. Rothenberg

A large part of my life revolves around my dad. Sometimes, I even feel a strong sense of connection, something very tangible when I learn something new in the martial arts.

—Brandon Lee on his father Bruce Lee

My dad worked me like a dog when I was a kid. From eight years old, I was an integral part of his business and working, and you know, made me.

—Jesse James, outlaw

He that does not bring up his son to some honest calling and employment brings him up to be a thief.

—Jewish proverb

I kind of was raised at The Comedy Store by comedians. When you see my dad on stage before me and then you see me, you'll see where I got a lot of my stuff.

—Pauly Shore

I talk to my dad all the time, he's more like my buddy than my father, and he's not happy that I use him in my act. But I tell him, I have to get something out of this.

—David Spade

Because he was a very funny guy [my father] was often asked to get up and speak at insurance conventions. I remember seeing him working on jokes, writing them out on big yellow pads. I was always fascinated to see where he'd cross out certain phrases, depending on what the audience would be like.

—Jay Leno

Mother was a concert singer; my father was an amateur comedian. He was pretty cute around the house, making jokes all the time.

—Bob Hope

When I auditioned for my high school band the band director was excited because my father was known to be a great musician. When he heard me, he said "Are you sure you're Ellis's son?"

—Wynton Marsalis

The worst misfortune that can happen to an ordinary man is to have an extraordinary father.

—Austin O'Malley

In the early years, I found a voice that was my voice and also partly my father's voice. But isn't that what you always do? Why do kids at five years old go into the closet and put their daddy's shoes on? Hey, my kids do it.

–Bruce Springsteen

[M]y father was an engineer and he helped to guide me into some science fair projects that were electronics, **so my love grew.**

—Steve Wozniak

> When I needed him to step up for me on the financial level, and I knew that he really didn't have it, my dad found a way to get it for me, because he knew it was important to me.

—Jimmy Smits on his father's support of his acting career

I must study politics and war that my sons may have liberty to study mathematics and philosophy. My sons ought to study mathematics and philosophy, geography, natural history, naval architecture, navigation, commerce, and agriculture in order to give their children a right to study painting, poetry, music, architecture, statuary, tapestry, and porcelain.

—John Adams

My dad was a guitar player, and he sang. He knew what he liked about music. He had a great memory, and he could show me things.

—Ricky Skaggs

My father . . . loved Broadway shows, and he would come home and approximate the songs on the piano, and he'd put his hands on the keys, and he'd put my hand, when I was tiny, on the melody, because he always played the melody with his little finger on the top. **And so that was my exposure to piano.**

—Stephen Sondheim

Dad bought me a toy drum one Christmas, and I eventually destroyed it. I wanted a real drum, and he bought me a snare drum. Dad continued to buy me one drum after the other.

—Keith Thibodeaux

What I do now is all my dad's fault, because he bought me a guitar as a boy, for no apparent reason.

—Rod Stewart

Until you have a son of your own . . . you will never know the sense of honor that makes a man want to be more than he is and to pass something good and hopeful into the hands of his son. And you will never know the heartbreak of the fathers who are haunted by the personal demons that keep them from being the men they want their sons to be.

—Kent Nerburn

[My father] had the poorest lemon ranch in California. I can assure you. He sold it before they found oil on it.

—Richard M. Nixon

My father was not a failure. After all, he was the father of a president of the United States.

—Harry S Truman

When I grew up, people said, "You'll never be the man your dad was." And I said, "Gee, I hope not."

—RIP TORN

I kind of rebelled against it. I resisted it. I didn't know what I wanted to do when I was a kid and was reluctant to go into, y'know, Dad's line of business.

—Jeff Bridges on his father Lloyd Bridges

SONS HAVE ALWAYS HAD A REBELLIOUS WISH TO BE DISILLUSIONED BY THAT WHICH CHARMED THEIR FATHERS.

—ALDOUS HUXLEY

So the day that I said, "I am going to USC Film School," my father looked at me and said, "You're going to go join the circus?" That was his quote. I said, "I want to be a movie director." And he said, "You're going to go join the circus." . . . And, of course, my mother's attitude was . . . "Let him get it out of his system."

—ROBERT ZEMECKIS

Father and son are natural enemies and each is happier and more secure in keeping it that way.

–John Steinbeck

[A]rchie is the bigger-than-life epitome of something that is in all of us, like it or not. Remember the line "You're the laziest white man I ever seen"? That line was my father's—addressed to me, more than once. And I used to accuse him of making racial slurs, and we'd get into real Mike-and-Archie shouting matches. And we were a middle-class *Jewish* family.

—Norman Lear on the character
Archie Bunker from *All in the Family*

I WOULD NEVER HAVE DONE WHAT I'D DONE IF I'D CONSIDERED MY FATHER AS SOMEBODY I WANTED TO PLEASE.

—ROBERT MAPPLETHORPE

A dramatic thing, **the first time you** stand up to your dad.

–Lenny Kravitz

CHIP OFF THE BLOCK

Several studies find a strong correlation between a father's intelligence and his son's— although the sons usually score higher in standardized IQ tests.

[T]he father-son relationship tests understanding and patience at least **as much as marriage does.**

—Alan Valentine

Father and I were enemies, open and avowed.
We conducted a series of skirmishes against one
another, he trying to steal my time with Mother
and I his.

—Frank O'Connor

A wise man maketh a glad father: but a foolish
son is the heaviness of his mother.

—Proverbs 10:1

[H]aving a son seems to disrupt a marriage
more than having a girl but, paradoxically, for
men a son seems to make it harder to leave the
marriage. They may be less happy, but they
don't leave; many say they have an obligation
to their son.

—David Cohen

Me and my father went through a war period where we wasn't talking. He wanted me to go to theology school—I didn't want to go. I wanted to do music. I told him I was a minister through music.

—Wyclef Jean

On the subject of your future pursuits we will converse when I see you and when you get home. It will be best for you to form no plans. Your mama and I have been thinking and planning for you. I shall disclose to you our plan when I see you. Till then, suspend your mind. . . .

—Reverend Jedidiah Morse to his son Samuel B. Morse

There must always be a struggle between a father and son, while one aims at power and the other at independence.

—Samuel Johnson

My mother approved, my father just didn't accept the idea of my being an actor. I think that's the reason he kept the hardware store in operation, because I think he was pretty sure that I was going to be found out sooner or later, and he wanted to have a job for me to come back to.

—James Stewart

A father follows the course of his son's life and notes many things of which he has not the privilege to speak.

—William Carlos Williams

Every son, at one point or another, defies his father, fights him, departs from him, only to return to him—if he is lucky—closer and more secure than before.

—Leonard Bernstein

you're not a man until your father says you're a man.

—Burt Reynolds

I didn't know the full facts of life until I was seventeen. My father never talked about his work.

—Martin Freud, on his father Sigmund Freud

My father taught me about the birds and bees.
He didn't know anything about girls.

—Joey Adams

My father told me all about the birds and the bees. The liar—I went steady with a woodpecker till I was twenty-one.

—Bob Hope

If you've never seen a real, fully developed look of disgust, just tell your son how you conducted yourself when you were a boy.

—Kin Hubbard

When I was a boy of fourteen, my father was so ignorant I could hardly stand to have the old man around. But when I got to be twenty-one, I was astonished at how much he had learned in seven years.

—Mark Twain (attr.)

Like Mark Twain, when I was young, I probably didn't appreciate my father at all. But thinking back, some of the things he did became so meaningful. I didn't realize at the time. For example, he tried to get across to us never try to be better than someone else. Learn from others and never cease trying to be the best you can be at whatever you're doing.

—John Wooden

My father didn't tell me how to live; he lived and let me watch him do it.

–Clarence B. Kelland

I never had a speech from my father "this is what you should or shouldn't do," but I just learned to be led by example. **My father wasn't perfect.**

—Adam Sandler

I talk and talk and talk, and I haven't taught people in fifty years what my father taught by example in one week.

–Mario Cuomo

I love my dad. He was never driven by greed, power, or glory.

—Charlie Sheen

I was influenced by my father, who, in the tiny village of Plains and the surrounding farming community, played a very vital role—in the church, he was on the local school board, he was on the local hospital authority. He had run for the legislature, served in the House of Representatives. . . . I saw that my daddy's life was very extensive and very valuable to people.

—JIMMY CARTER

I expect I must, in part, have developed my notion of character from watching my father struggle against the mesquite.

–Larry McMurtry

My father . . . named me Carlos after a brother he lost—a very brilliant young man who died at twenty-one. . . . He was an intellectual. I think my father wanted to see his brother in me, so he put books into my hands at a very early age. He fostered my literary and artistic inclinations. So he was my best teacher.

—Carlos Fuentes

The father who does not teach his son his duties is equally guilty with the son who neglects them.

—Confucius

My father was always giving me lessons about how to deal with the difficulties of life. I guess he had a real sense that you've got to prepare your children—not only for the good things that are going to happen in life—but the bad and difficult things, because nobody gets through life without difficult things happening. **We all have to know how to handle crisis.**

— **Rudolph Giuliani**

One of the scary things is that, when you're a kid, you look at your dad as the man who has no fear. When you're an adult, you realize your father had fear, and that you have it, too.

—David Duchovny

My father taught me how to reason, how to reach my mind. My soul belonged to my grandfather and my mother. They influenced me profoundly, to this day. When I write, I have the feeling, literally, physically, that one of them is behind my back, looking over my shoulder and reading what I'm writing. I'm terribly afraid of their judgment.

—Elie Wiesel

[I] sat in a leather chair in the office of a Jungian analyst once or twice a week for a number of years . . . [describing] my difficulties with my mother, while he replied, **"I think you have more issues with your father."**

—Alec Wilkinson

I cheat my boys every chance I get.

It makes 'em sharp.

—William Rockefeller,
father of John D. Rockefeller

♛

This thought lately, that as a little child I had been defeated by my father and because of ambition have never been able to quit the battlefield all these years despite the perpetual defeats I suffer.

—Franz Kafka

The one thing I remember about Christmas was that my father used to take me out in a boat about ten miles offshore on Christmas Day, and I used to have to swim back. Extraordinary. It was a ritual. Mind you, that wasn't the hard part. The difficult bit was getting out of the sack.

—John Cleese

Perhaps host and guest is really the happiest relation for father and son.

–Evelyn Waugh

I'd turned out to be a skinny little kid. I still only weighed about nine pounds when I was fifteen, so I didn't live up to my father's expectations. He felt embarrassed by it, so it embarrassed me too.

—Peter Fonda

I never got along with my dad. Kids used to come up to me and say, "My dad can beat up your dad." I'd say, "Yeah? When?"

—Bill Hicks

I remember the time I was kidnapped, and they sent a piece of my finger to my father. He said he wanted more proof.

—Rodney Dangerfield

He was the type of man who never worked for you. He was your father. I never went in and said, "Dad, do this" or "Do that." I'd go in and say, "Dad, what do you think about this? What can we do?" I really needed him.

—George Steinbrenner

A boy wants something very special from his father. You hear it said that fathers want their sons to be what they feel they cannot themselves be, but I tell you it also works the other way. I know that as a small boy I wanted my father to be a certain thing he was not. **I wanted him to be a proud, silent, dignified father.**

—Sherwood Anderson

MY DAD HAS ALWAYS BEEN THE BOHEMIAN.

—Leonardo DiCaprio

My dad loved to laugh. He was very funny and very silly.

—Mike Myers

My dad was the town drunk. **Most of the time that's not so bad; but New York City?**
                                        —Henny Youngman

There's sometimes a weird benefit to having an alcoholic, violent father. He really motivated me in that I never wanted to be anything like him.
                                        —Dean Koontz

I grew up not liking my father very much. I never saw him cry. But he must have. **Everybody cries.**
                                        —Charley Pride

My father was the guy on the block who said hi to everyone.
                                        —Damon Wayans

My father is my idol, so I always did everything like him. He used to work two jobs and still come home happy every night. He didn't do drugs or drink, and he wouldn't let anyone smoke in his house. Those are the rules I adopted, too.

—EARVIN "MAGIC" JOHNSON

It is not flesh and blood, **but the heart which makes us fathers and sons.**

—Johann von Schiller

This is the moment that I deeply wish my parents could have lived to share. My father would have enjoyed what you have so generously said of me— and my mother would have believed it.

—Lyndon B. Johnson giving commencement address at Baylor University in 1965

I decided in my life that I would do nothing that did not reflect positively on my father's life.

—Sidney Poitier

Sons are for fathers the twice-told tale.

—Victoria Secunda

A man knows when he is growing old because he begins to look like his father.

—Gabriel Garcia Marquez

I looked in the mirror and saw my father's face on my body.

—Sammy Davis, Jr.

I don't mind looking into the mirror and seeing my father.

—Michael Douglas

God's Gifts to Children: Grandfathers

Never have children, only grandchildren.

—GORE VIDAL

I've got a vision now. I've been president of the United States, and my vision is being the best grandfather in the entire world.

—George H. W. Bush

There are fathers who do not love their children; there is no grand-father who does not adore his grandson.

—VICTOR HUGO

There is nothing like having grandchildren to restore your faith in heredity.

—Doug Larson

The reason grandchildren and grandparents **get along so well is that** they have a common enemy.

–Sam Levenson

EVERY GENERATION REVOLTS AGAINST ITS FATHERS AND MAKES FRIENDS WITH ITS GRANDFATHERS.

—LEWIS MUMFORD

> I met my grandfather just before he died, and it was the first time that I had seen Dad with a relative of his. It was interesting to see my own father as a son and the body language and alteration in attitude that comes with that, and it sort of changed our relationship for the better.

—Christian Bale

It's one of nature's ways that we often feel closer to distant generations than to the generation immediately preceding us.

—Igor Stravinsky

The average man will bristle if you say his father was dishonest, but he will brag a little if he discovers that his great-grandfather was a pirate.

—Bern Williams

Our children are here to stay, but our babies and toddlers and preschoolers are gone as fast as they can grow up—and we have only a short moment with each. When you see a grand-father take a baby in his arms, you see that the moment hasn't always been long enough.

—S. ADAMS SULLIVAN

What children need most are the essentials that grandparents provide in abundance. They give unconditional love, kindness, patience, humor, comfort, lessons in life. And, most importantly, cookies.

—Rudolph Giuliani

Dad liked to have his family around him.
When my children were small, they spent many
weekends at Granny and Grandpa's. They played
their games all around him, and sometimes on
him, while he did his homework.

—Diane Disney Miller on her father Walt Disney

Few things are more delightful than
grandchildren fighting over your lap.

—Doug Larson

The best babysitters, of course, are the baby's
grandparents. You feel completely comfortable
entrusting your baby to them for long periods,
which is why most grandparents flee to Florida.

—Dave Barry

Of course, many people say that grandparents get all the fun of parenting with none of the responsibility, but I have my own theory. It has been scientifically proven that testosterone levels in men start falling in their late twenties, so the authoritarian enforcer we knew as kids mellows over time and becomes the kindly, doting grandfather.

—Conan O'Brien

When grandparents enter the door, discipline flies out the window.
—Ogden Nash

When I was little, my grandfather used to make me stand in a closet for five minutes without moving. He said it was elevator practice.

—Steven Wright

UNDER ONE ROOF

According to the U.S. Census Bureau, approximately 1.7 million American grandfathers live with one or more of their grandchildren.

I don't intentionally spoil my grandkids. It's just that correcting them often takes more energy than I have left.

—Gene Perret

The simplest toy, one which even the youngest child can operate, is called a grandparent.

—Sam Levenson

Nobody can do for little children what grandparents do. Grandparents sort of sprinkle stardust over the lives of little children.

—ALEX HALEY

Grandfather knows that after the fun and games are over with his adorable grandchildren he can return to the quiet of his own home and peacefully reflect on this phenomenon of fatherhood.

—Alvin F. Poussaint, MD

Does Grandpa love to babysit his grandchildren? Are you kidding? By day he is too busy taking hormone shots at the doctor's or chip shots on the golf course. At night he and Grandma are too busy doing the cha-cha.

—Hal Boyle

My grandfather was a very elegant individual. My father also. He was a lawyer and farmer in Cuba. In Miami, he had to go to work wherever he could. But whenever it was time to go out, you saw how they cared for how they looked.

—ANDY GARCIA

MY GRANDFATHER FRANK LLOYD WRIGHT WORE A RED SASH ON HIS WEDDING NIGHT. THAT IS GLAMOUR!

—ANNE BAXTER

I don't mind being a grandfather; I've been a mother for so many years. You just can't believe what it's like being a father. Especially when you come out of the chaos of the road to getting married and having children.

–Steven Tyler

Grandchildren don't make a man feel old; it's the knowledge that he's married to a grandmother.

—G. Norman Collie

Who wants to be married to a grandfather?

–Loretta Lynn

I'm so lucky to be a father and a grandfather and to actually see them growing up and having children—it's quite amazing.

—CRAIG T. NELSON

By the time the **youngest children** have learned to keep the house tidy, the oldest grandchildren are on hand to tear **it to pieces.**

—Christopher Morley

I am Father, and I am Grandfather. So there is two love.

—LUCIANO PAVAROTTI

perfect love sometimes does not come until grandchildren are born.

—Welsh proverb

Being grandparents sufficiently removes us from the responsibilities **so that we can be friends.**

—Allan Frome

More and more, when I single out the person who inspired me most, I go back to my grandfather . . . because he taught me the value of being able to listen, not to rush to judgment, being really rational.

—James Earl Jones

> [I]t was rare to find an uneducated rural southerner without a racist bone in his body. That's exactly what my grandfather was. I could see that black people looked different, but because he treated them like he did everybody else, asking after their children and about their work, I thought they were just like me.

—Bill Clinton

My grandfather once told me

that there are two kinds of people: those who work and those who take the credit. He told me to try to be in the first group; there was less competition there.

—Indira Gandhi

You've got to do your own growing, no matter how tall your grandfather was.
–Irish proverb

My grandfather gave me my first guitar, an old acoustic with palm trees and dancing girls painted on it.

—Dan Fogelberg

What is it about grandparents that is so lovely? I'd like to say that grandparents are God's gifts to children. And if they can but see, hear, and feel what these people have to give, they can mature at a fast rate.

—Bill Cosby

My role model was my grandfather. He instilled in me the feeling that no matter how successful you are, you have a responsibility to help others.

—Kevin Johnson

I was taught by my grandfather that anything that your mind can conceive, you can have. It's a reality.

—Lenny Kravitz

I phoned my grandparents and my grandfather said, "We saw your movie." "Which one?" I said. He shouted, "Betty, what was the name of that movie I didn't like?"

—Brad Pitt

keepinG TIme

Properly known as a "longcase clock," the floor-standing pendulum clock usually six to eight feet tall came to be known as a "grandfather clock" after the popular song, "My Grandfather's Clock," written in 1876 by British songwriter Henry Clay Work.

I like to do nice things for my grandchildren—like buy them those toys I've always wanted to play with.

—Gene Perret

My grandfather taught me gen-
erosity. He sold snow cones in Harlem.
I went with him at five, and he let me hand
out the change and snow cones. I learned a
lot in the couple of years that we did that.

—ERIK ESTRADA

I told them that my grandfather had died in
the Great Crash of 1929—a stockbroker jumped
out of a window and crushed him and his
pushcart down below.

—Mario Cuomo

My grandfather had a wonderful funeral. My grandfather was a very insignificant man, actually. At his funeral his hearse *followed* the other cars. It was a nice funeral, though, you would have liked it. It was a catered funeral. It was held in a big hall with accordion players. On the buffet table there was a replica of the deceased in potato salad.

—WOODY ALLEN

Just because someone's dead doesn't mean it's over. My grandfather died more than twenty-five years ago, but I still think of him a lot and smell his smell.

—Julian Clary

My grandfather was a voodoo priest.
A lot of my life dealt with spirituality. I can close
my eyes and remember where I come from.
—Wyclef Jean

Elephants and grandchildren never forget.
—Andy Rooney

POSTERITY IS THE
PATRIOTIC NAME FOR
GRANDCHILDREN.
—ART LINKLETTER

Look Her Straight in the Eyes: Wisdom from Dad

When you teach your son,
you teach your son's son.
–The Talmud

Drummed into me, above all, by my dad, by the whole family, was that without your good name, you would be nothing.

—Arthur Ashe

How true Daddy's words were when he said: "All children must look after their own upbringing." Parents can only give good advice or put them on the right paths, but the final forming of a person's character lies in their own hands.

—Anne Frank

My father always said there are four things a child needs: plenty of love, nourishing food, regular sleep, and lots of soap and water. After that, what he needs most is some intelligent neglect.

—Ivy Baker Priest

The important thing, I learned from my father, was to find your own bone and sink your teeth into it.

—William Plummer

I got a note from my father, who said that "Success is wonderful if you don't inhale." That was his own aphorism, and I think it's the very best thing he could have said to me or anyone else on the subject.

—Sam Waterston

Man With The Answers

The aphorism "Father knows best" first appeared in print as a headline in the May 2, 1924, edition of the *Los Angeles Times*.

My father said: "You must never try to make all the money that's in a deal. Let the other fellow make some money too, because if you have a reputation for always making all the money, you won't have many deals."

—J. Paul Getty

THIS ABOVE ALL: TO THINE OWN SELF BE TRUE, AND IT MUST FOLLOW, AS THE NIGHT THE DAY, THOU CANST NOT THEN BE FALSE TO ANY MAN.

— POLONIUS TO HIS SON LAERTES IN
Hamlet BY WILLIAM SHAKESPEARE

♛

My father always used to say that when you die, if you've got five real friends, then you've had a great life.

—Lee Iacocca

[My father] had street smarts and street ethics. He hated bullies and despised cheats. He always taught me the following: **"Always fight up, never fight down."** He meant that I should always fight with people who are more powerful, more influential, and stronger than I am. "It's better to lose to a better fighter than to beat a poorer one," he would say.

—Alan Dershowitz

My father told me there's no difference between a black snake and a white snake. They both bite.

—Thurgood Marshall

My dad always used to tell me that if they challenge you to an after-school fight, tell them you won't wait—you can kick their ass right now.

—Cameron Diaz

MIND YOU, DON'T GO LOOKING FOR FIGHTS, BUT IF YOU FIND YOUR-SELF IN ONE, MAKE DAMN SURE YOU WIN.

—CLYDE MORRISON, TO HIS SON JOHN WAYNE

It's very important to lose graciously.
My dad taught me that.

—Jack Nicklaus

When I was eleven years old, my father told me, "There's one thing you can do in your lifetime that will be free and cost you nothing, and that is to be nice to people."

—Sparky Anderson

Father told me that if I ever met a lady in a dress like yours, **I must look her straight in the eyes.**

—Charles, Prince of Wales
to a woman in a low-cut dress

Boy, was my father right when he said to me:

"Don't marry anyone who cannot make you laugh."

—Joanna Barnes

My dad taught me true words
you have to use in every relationship.

Yes, baby.

—Star Jones

Father taught us that opportunity
and responsibility go hand in hand. I think
we all act on that principle, on the basic
human impulse that makes a man want to
make the best of what's in him and what's
been given him.

—LAURENCE ROCKEFELLER

My father used to say, "Let them see you
and not the suit. That should be secondary."

–Cary Grant

[My father] told me that if a man had unshined
shoes, it reflected poorly on him. His shoes always
had a shine you could adjust your tie in.

—Al Roker

WISDOM OF THE AIRWAVES

Father Knows Best, brainchild of series star Robert Young, debuted as a radio situation comedy in 1949 and made a seamless transition to television, where it ran until 1963. Over the years, it appeared on all three major television networks.

I have never been a material girl. My father always told me never to love anything that cannot love you back.

—Imelda Marcos

The best money advice ever given to me was from my father. When I was a little girl, he told me, "Don't spend anything unless you have to."

—Dinah Shore

👑

MY FATHER ALWAYS TOLD ME, "FIND A JOB YOU LOVE AND YOU'LL NEVER HAVE TO WORK A DAY IN YOUR LIFE."

—JIM FOX

[W]hat a gift to be able to go into your dad's line of work . . . with all the joy and excitement of getting paid to do something you love so much.

—Bonnie Raitt

Daddy taught us how to work hard, to be your own person, to be strong. And my daddy's handshake was better than a document that had all the seals on it.

—Reba McEntire

My father was very sure about certain matters pertaining to the universe. To him, all good things—trout as well as eternal salvation—come by grace and grace comes by art, and art does not come easy.

—Norman Maclean

We used to have to watch the news as a family every night. . . . My father said, "You should always know what's going on in the world, and the news changes every day."

—Gayle King

My father used to say that we must surrender our youth to purchase wisdom. What he never told me was how badly we get cheated on the exchange rate.

– Morris West

I could just remember how my father used to say that the reason for living was to get ready to stay dead a long time.

—WILLIAM FAULKNER

[My father] taught me that **watermelon is the Happy Fruit.** He always used to tell me, "Son, if you're ever suicidally depressed or at the end of your rope, just go out and find a nice ripe watermelon, then throw it down on the floor and cram as much of it in your mouth as you possibly can. It'll cheer you right up." **And you know what? It does.**

—Al Yankovic

Selected Biographical Notes

Andre Agassi (b. 1970), U.S. tennis star and Olympic gold medal winner.

Margaret Atwood (b. 1939), Canadian novelist and poet, recipient of the Booker Prize.

Joan Baez (b. 1941), American folksinger, songwriter, and political activist.

James Baldwin (1924–1987), U.S. writer and civil rights activist.

Dave Barry (b. 1947), author and humorist; recipient of Pulitzer Prize.

Mikhail Baryshnikov (b. 1948), Russian-born dancer, choreographer, and international ballet star.

Yogi Berra (b. 1925), former Major League baseball player and manager known for his slips of tongue.

Josh Billings (1818–1885), American humorist known for folksy wisdom.

Robert Bly (b. 1926), poet, writer, and activist in the men's movement in the United States.

Erma Bombeck (1927–1996), humor columnist who specialized in observations of family life.

Dr. Joyce Brothers (b. 1928), psychologist and author.

Heywood Broun (1888–1939), journalist and sportswriter.

David Cohen (b. 1946), psychologist, filmmaker, editor of *Psychology News,* and author of *The Father's Book.*

Sean "Diddy" Combs (b. 1969), rap artist, record producer, and clothing designer.

Bill Cosby (b. 1937), actor, comedian, television producer, and activist for children's education.

Imogen Cunningham (1883–1976), American photographer.

Mario Cuomo (b. 1932), U.S. politician and former governor of New York.

Roald Dahl (1916–1990), Welsh writer of adult and children's books, including *Charlie and the Chocolate Factory.*

Johnny Depp (b. 1963), U.S. actor known for unconventional roles.

Cameron Diaz (b. 1972), one of the most highly paid U.S. actresses.

Umberto Eco (b. 1932), Italian novelist and philosopher.

Havelock Ellis (1859–1939), British doctor, sexual psychologist and social reformer.

Jeff Foxworthy (b. 1958), American comedian and game show host known for redneck humor.

Anna Freud (1895–1982), psychoanalyst and daughter of Sigmund Freud.

Robert Frost (1874–1963), American poet, four-time winner of Pulitzer Prize for Poetry.

Indira Gandhi (1917–1984), former prime minister of India.

Bill Gates (b. 1955), co-founder and chairman of Microsoft and noted philanthropist.

Rudolph Giuliani (b. 1944), politician and former mayor of New York City was named "Person of the Year" in 2001 by *Time* magazine.

Doris Kearns Goodwin (b. 1943), Pulitzer Prize–winning author and historian.

Bob Greene (b. 1947), journalist, columnist, and author of several books including *Good Morning, Merry Sunshine.*

Lillian Hellman (1905-1984), American playwright and progressive political activist.

James Hetfield (b. 1963), songwriter, vocalist, and guitarist for heavy metal band Metallica.

Lee Iacocca (b. 1924), U.S. business leader and author.

Enrique Iglesias (b. 1975), Spanish singing sensation.

John Irving (b. 1942), U.S. novelist and screenwriter.

Wyclef Jean (b. 1972), Haitian-American rap artist, guitarist, and record producer.

Janis Joplin (1943-1970), influential rock star of the 1960s.

James Joyce (1882-1941), Irish novelist and poet.

Garrison Keillor (b. 1942), author, humorist, and radio personality.

Harmon Killebrew (b. 1936), former Major League baseball player and broadcaster.

Gayle King (b. 1954), television personality and editor-at-large for *O, The Oprah Magazine.*

Larry King, (b. 1933), host of *Larry King Live* on CNN, editor of the book *My Dad & Me.*

Lenny Kravitz (b. 1964), Grammy Award–winning singer and songwriter.

Matt Lauer (b. 1957), co-host of *The Today Show.*

Norman Lear (b. 1922), American television writer and producer.

Jay Leno (b. 1950), Emmy Award–winning comedian who hosts *The Tonight Show.*

Robert Lowell (1917–1977), American poet, winner of Pulitzer Prize for Poetry.

Douglas MacArthur (1880–1964), American general and Medal of Honor recipient.

Wynton Marsalis (b. 1961), Grammy Award–winning trumpeter and composer, received first Pulitzer Prize for Music for a jazz recording.

Willie Mays (b. 1931), Hall of Fame baseball player.

Margaret Mead (1901–1978), author and cultural anthropologist.

Arthur Miller (1915–2005), Pulitzer Prize–winning American playwright.

Conan O'Brien (b. 1963), Emmy Award–winning comedian who hosts *Late Night with Conan O'Brien.*

Mark O'Connell, PhD (b. 1954), psychotherapist, faculty member of Harvard Medical School, and author of *The Good Father*.

Bobby Orr (b. 1948), National Hockey League star, member of Hockey Hall of Fame.

Joe Orton (1933-1967), British playwright.

Kevin Osborn (b. 1959), author of *The Complete Idiot's Guide to Fatherhood*.

Rafael Palmeiro (b. 1964), Major League baseball player born in Cuba.

Dr. Kyle Pruett (b. 1943), Director of Medical Studies, Yale Child Study Center.

Bonnie Raitt (b. 1949), Grammy Award–winning guitarist and vocalist; daughter of Broadway musical legend John Raitt.

Paul Reiser (b. 1957), comedian, actor, and author of several books, including *Babyhood*.

Ann Richards (1933–2006), politician and former Texas governor.

Cokie Roberts (b. 1943), American journalist, author, and radio and television commentator.

Al Roker (b. 1954), weather anchor of *The Today Show* and author of several books including *Big Shoes: In Celebration of Dads and Fatherhood.*

Adam Sandler (b. 1966), comedian, actor, and former cast member of *Saturday Night Live.*

Anne Sexton (1928–1974), American poet and author of children's books.

Quinton Skinner (b. 1969), novelist and author of memoir *Do I Look Like a Daddy to You?*

Gloria Steinem (b. 1934), feminist activist and author; co-founder of *Ms.* magazine

Adlai E. Stevenson (1900–1965), U.S. politician, presidential candidate, and ambassador to the United Nations.

Jon Stewart (b. 1962), comedian and writer; host of *The Daily Show* on Comedy Central.

Paul Tsongas (1941–1997), U.S. Senator and representative from Massachusetts who ran for president in 1992.

Liv Tyler (b. 1977), actress and daughter of Aerosmith lead singer Steven Tyler.

Alan Valentine (1901–1980), former president of the University of Rochester and editor of *Fathers to Sons.*

Oscar Wilde (1854–1900), Irish playwright, poet, and novelist known for his wit.

Alec Wilkinson (b. 1952), author and staff writer for *The New Yorker.*

Venus Williams (b. 1980), U.S. professional tennis player known for the speed of her serve.

John Wooden (b. 1910), former U.S. basketball coach; led UCLA to ten NCAA National Championships.

Steve Wozniak (b. 1950), co-founder of Apple Computer.

General Chuck Yeager (b. 1923), U.S. Air Force test pilot who was the first to travel faster than sound.

Frank Zappa (1940–1993), composer and musician best known for his work in the band The Mothers of Invention.

Robert Zemeckis (b. 1952), film director, received Best Director Academy Award for *Forrest Gump.*

Index

A

Abdul-Jabbar, Kareem, 51

Adams, Franklin P., 124

Adams, James T., 175

Adams, Joey, 228

Adams, John, 216

Addison, Joseph, 153

Agassi, Andre, 49, 193

Aldrin, Buzz, 203

Ali, Muhammad, x, 49

Allen, Tim, 89

Allen, Woody, 261

Anderson, Sherwood, 239

Anderson, Sparky, 270

Annenberg, Walter, 67

Ashe, Arthur, 264

Asner, Ed, 121

Atwood, Margaret, x, 25

B

Bacon, Francis, 99

Baez, Joan, 176

Bagnold, Enid, 181

Baldwin, James, 208

Bale, Christian, 246

Bales, Susan Ford, 159

Barclay, Dorothy, 93

Barnes, Joanna, 271

Barry, Dave, 80, 93, 248

Baryshnikov, Mikhail, 71

Baxter, Anne, 252

Bergen, Candace, 20

Berle, Milton, 80

Bernstein, Leonard, 227

Berra, Dale, 210

Berra, Yogi, 17, 186, 190

Berry, Halle, 178

Bible, 2, 136, 144, 146, 225

Billings, Josh, 120, 123

Bishop, Jim, 173

Bly, Robert, 22, 73, 109, 164

Blyth, Myrna, 178

Bombeck, Erma, 26

Bonaduce, Danny, 136

Bort, Julie, 128

Boyle, Hal, 251

Brady, Tom, 39

Bratt, Benjamin, 154

Brenton, Myron, 65

Breton, Nicholas, 135

Bridges, Jeff, 220

Brock, Lou, 106

Brock, Peter, 74

Brothers, Joyce, 160

Broun, Heywood, 53, 85

Brown, H. Jackson, 32

Brown, John Gregory, 154

Browning, Elizabeth
    Barrett, 163

Burritt, Elihu, 134

Burroughs, John, 133

Busch, Wilhelm, 2

Bush, George H. W., 244

Butler, Brett, 166

Buttons, Red, 147

C

Cadogan, William, 95

Carter, Hodding, 130

Carter, Jimmy, 232

Cash, Rosanne, 182

Charles, Prince of Wales, 270

Child, Lydia Maria, 7

Ciccone, Madonna, 169

Clark, Frank A., 81

Clary, Julian, 261

Cleese, John, 237

Clinton, Bill, 35, 208, 256

Cohen, David, 29, 225

Cole, Nat King, 37

Collie, G. Norman, 253

Combs, Sean "Diddy," 175

Como, Perry, 119

Confucius, 233

Coolidge, Calvin, 76

Cosby, Bill, 35, 60, 81, 85, 112, 115, 140, 171, 257

Courtney, Margaret, 24

Crisp, Quentin, 146

Cunningham, Imogen, 161

Cuomo, Mario, 231, 260

D

Dahl, Roald, 114

Damon, Matt, 48

Dangerfield, Rodney, 238

Davis, Sammy Jr., 45, 242

Day, Clarence, 109, 135

de la Fontaine, Jean, 30

de Montaigne, Michel, 137

Depp, Johnny, 58, 150

Dershowitz, Alan, 268

De Vries, Peter, 56, 111

Diaz, Cameron, 157, 269

DiCaprio, Leonardo, 239

Dickens, Charles, 16, 25, 77

Dietrich, Marlene, 47

Dillon, Matt, 73

Dobson, James, 111

Dodge, Mary Mapes, 111

Donne, Oliva, 61

Douglas, James, 99

Douglas, Michael, 242

Draxe, Thomas, 209

Duchovny, David, 234

E

Eco, Umberto, 17

Edwards, Anthony, xi, 69

Ellis, Havelock, 27

Ellison, Katherine, 43, 84

Elway, Jack, 192

Espy, Hilda Cole, 102

Estrada, Erik, 260

Euripides, 180

Evans, Richard L., 203

F

Faber, Frederick W., 13, 117

Fadiman, Clifton, 104

Faulkner, William, 277

Feiffer, Jules, 210

Felson, Henry George, x, 39

Fielding, Henry, 123

Figes, Eva, 77

Firkins, Oscar W., 62

Fitzgerald, Edward, 77

Fogelberg, Dan, 257

Fonda, Henry, 170

Fonda, Peter, 70, 237

Ford, Gerald R., 159

Ford, Harrison, 68

Fox, Jim, 274

Fox, Michael J., 51, 106

Fox, Susan, 97

Foxworthy, Jeff, 18

Foyt, A. J., 199

Frank, Anne, 153, 265

Franzen, Jonathan, 72

Freud, Anna, xiii, 156

Freud, Martin, 228

Freud, Sigmund, 9, 105

Frey, Glenn, 42

Frome, Allan, 255

Fromm, Erich, 27

Frost, Robert, 13

Fuentes, Carlos, 233

Fulghum, Robert, 119

G

Gandhi, Indira, 168, 256

Garcia, Andy, 252

Garner, Cindy, 5

Garretty, Marion C., 106

Gates, Bill, 15

Genevie, Louis, 19, 89

Getty, J. Paul, 266

Gibran, Kahlil, 60

Giuliani, Rudolph, xiii, 234, 247

Goethe, Johann Wolfgang von, 107, 202

Goldman, Marcus Jacob, 38

Goodman, Ellen, 23

Goodwin, Doris Kearns, 189

Gosse, Edmund, 10

Graham, Billy, 26

Graham, Harry, 138

Grant, Cary, 272

Greene, Bob, 40, 53, 69, 96, 126

Groening, Matt, ix, 46

H

Haley, Alex, 251

Hall, Donald, xi, 185

Handey, Jack, 125

Harden, Marcia Gay, 161

Hargrave, Terry, 156

Harwell, Ernie, 184

Hayes, Helen, 152

Hearn, Lafcadio, 34

Hellman, Lillian, 166

Helps, Arthur, 148

Hemingway, Ernest, 90

Hepburn, Thomas, 162

Herbert, George, 16

Hesburgh, Theodore M., 88

Hetfield, James, 52

Hicks, Bill, 238

Hobson, Laura Z., 104

Hoffman, Dustin, 68, 127

Holbrook, Hal, 70

Holmes, John Andrew, 129

Homer, 209

Hope, Bob, 56, 214, 229

Horowitz, Michael, 34, 116

Hoyt, Dick, 187

Hoyt, Rick, 187

Hubbard, Kim, 229

Hugo, Victor, 244

Hull, Bobby, 198

Hunter, Rachel, 172

Hurt, William, 53

Huxley, Aldous, 221

I

Iacocca, Lee, 267

Ice Cube, 118

Iglesias, Enrique, 209

Irving, John, 207

J

Jackson, Jesse, xi, 81

James, Henry Sr., 55

James, Jesse, 212

James, William, 57

Jarrell, Mary, 17

Jean, Wyclef, 226, 262

Jeter, Derek, 188

Jewett, Sarah Orne, 155

John Paul XXIII, 7

Johnson, Earvin "Magic," 241

Johnson, Kevin, 258

Johnson, Lyndon B., 241

Johnson, Samuel, 226

Jones, Chuck, 98

Jones, James Earl, 255

Jones, Star, 271

Jonson, Ben, 209

Joplin, Janis, 110

Josefowitz, Natasha, 182

Joubert, Joseph, 143

Joyce, James, 10

K

Kafka, Franz, 125, 236

Kassebaum, Nancy Landon, 169

Keillor, Garrison, 122, 151

Kelland, Clarence B., 230

Killebrew, Harmon, 185

King George VI, 179

King, Gayle, 152, 276

King, Larry, 8, 207

Kinski, Nastassja, 155

Koizumi, Kazuo, 144

Koontz, Dean, 240

Kravitz, Lenny, 223, 258

L

Lamarr, Hedy, 176

Lamb, Charles, 176

Larson, Doug, 245, 248

Lauer, Matt, 48

Lear, Norman, 222

Lee, Brandon, 211

Lennon, John, 91

Lennon, Julian, 91

Lennon, Sean, 91

Leno, Jay, 133, 213

Lerner, Max, 79, 206

Levenson, Sam, 56, 245, 250

Lewis, Jerry, 124

Lincoln, Abraham, 74

Linkletter, Art, 262

Lithgow, John, 115

Lodge, David, 37

Lombardo, Guy, 174

London, Jeremy, 45

Longfellow, Henry Wadsworth, xii, 55, 147

Lowell, Robert, 31

Lucci, Susan, 177

Lynd, Robert, 101, 126

Lynn, Loretta, 177, 253

M

MacArthur, Douglas, 57

MacLachlan, Kyle, 124, 196

Maclean, Norman, 275

Malkovitch, John, 151, 190

Mantle, Mickey, 186

Mapplethorpe, Robert, 223

Marcos, Imelda, 273

Margolies, Eva, 19, 89

Marquez, Gabriel Garcia, 242

Marquis, Don, 118, 139

Marsalis, Wynton, 214

Marshall, Thurgood, 268

Martin, Steve, 46, 179

Marx, Harpo, 44

Maugham, W. Somerset, 90

Mays, Willie, 188

McCartney, Paul, 79

McCourt, Frank, 32

McEntire, Reba, 275

McGinley, Phyllis, 174

McLaughlin, Mignon, 34

McMurtry, Larry, 59, 232

Mead, Margaret, ix, 3

Miller, Arthur, 61

Miller, Diane Disney, 248

Miller, Henry, 117

Minnelli, Liza, 160

Morley, Christopher, 254

Morrison, Clyde, 269

Morse, Jedediah, 226

Mountbatten, Lord, xii, 143

Mozart, Wolfgang Amadeus, 10

Mumford, Lewis, 245

Myers, Mike, 239

N

Nash, Ogden, 127, 249

Naylor, Gloria, 181

Nelson, Craig T., 254

Nerburn, Kent, 219

Nicklaus, Jack, 270

Nietzsche, Friedrich Wilhelm, 22, 210

Nin, Anaïs, 164

Nixon, Richard M., 219

Norman, Geoffrey, 40

O

O'Brien, Conan, 36, 142, 249

O'Connell, Mark, 43, 46, 58, 116, 140

O'Connor, Carroll, 14

O'Connor, Frank, 225

O'Malley, Austin, 214

O'Neal, Tatum, 163

O'Neill, Hugh, 94, 100

O'Rourke, P. J., 130, 142

Olinghouse, Lane, 120

Orben, Robert, 12

Orr, Bobby, 198

Orton, Joe, 2

Osborn, Kevin, 5

Osgood, Charles, 94

P

Palmeiro, Rafael, 184

Palmer, Arnold, 196

Pavarotti, Luciano, 254

Peguy, Charles, 147

Penn, William, 78, 123

Perret, Gene, 250, 259

Petrash, Jack, 15, 200

Petty, Adam, 28

Pflock, Aviva, 128

Pierce, David Hyde, 197

Piersall, Jimmy, 86

Pitt, Brad, 47, 258

Plummer, William, 266

Poitier, Sidney, 242

Poulter, Stephan B., 29, 74, 128

Poussaint, Alvin F., 251

Powys, Llewelyn, 3

Presley, Lisa Marie, 167

Pride, Charley, 240

Priest, Ivy Baker, 266

Priestley, J. B., 103

Pruett, Kyle, 97, 121

Q

Quinn, Anthony, 37

R

Rainier, Prince, 47

Raitt, Bonnie, 275

Reagan, Ron, 98

Reagan, Ronald, 205

Reiser, Paul, 45

Renkel, Ruth E., 82

Renner, Devra, 128

Reynolds, Burt, 228

Richards, Ann, 156

Richter, Jean Paul, 129

Rivera, Geraldo, 61

Roberts, Cokie, 168

Rock, Kid, 50

Rockefeller, Laurence, 272

Rockefeller, William, 236

Roker, Al, 95, 272

Rooney, Andy, 262

Roosevelt, Eleanor, 92

Roosevelt, Theodore, 170, 191

Rosemond, J., 139

Rothenberg, Michael B., 211

Rushdie, Salman, 208

Russell, Bertrand, 28, 197

Ryder, Winona, 173

S

Salinger, J. D., 112

Sanders, Deion, 52

Sandler, Adam, 50, 100, 231

Saroyan, William, 49

Sartre, Jean Paul, 8

Savalas, Telly, 78

Scacchi, Greta, 170

Schieffer, Bob, 41

Schirra, Walter M. Sr., 204

Scott, Walter, 62

Seles, Monica, 193

Sexton, Anne, 182

Shakespeare, William, xii, 118, 180, 201, 267

Shandling, Garry, 110

Shanley, Mary Kay, 20

Shaw, George Bernard, 16, 108, 148

Sheen, Charlie, 75, 231

Shelton, Sandi Kahn, 24, 67, 92, 96

Shields, Brooke, 195

Shore, Dinah, 274

Shore, Pauly, 212

Sinor, John, 172

Skaggs, Ricky, 217

Skelton, Red, 121

Skinner, Quinton, 7, 59, 150

Smiley, Jane, 31

Smith, Will, 52

Smits, Jimmy, 216

Sondheim, Stephen, 217

Sorvino, Mira, 162

Spade, David, 213

Spock, Benjamin, 86, 101, 211

Springsteen, Bruce, 215

Stanton, Elizabeth Cady, 167

Stark, Freya, 25

Stein, Gertrude, 206

Steinbeck, John, 222

Steinbrenner, George, 238

Steinem, Gloria, 65

Sterne, Laurence, 4

Stevenson, Adlai E., x, 21, 68, 120

Stewart, James, 227

Stewart, John, 41

Stewart, Rod, 218

Stone, Sharon, 157

Straus, Murray, 138

Stravinsky, Igor, 246

Strindberg, August, 75

Sullivan, S. Adams, 14, 42, 105,
    128, 247

T

Tagore, Rabindranath, 122

Talmud, 264

Thatcher, Margaret, 155

Thibodeaux, Keith, 218

Thompson, Dorothy, 9

Tolstoy, Leo, 36

Torn, Rip, 220

Truman, Harry S, 117, 181, 220

Tsongas, Paul, 82

Turnbull, Margaret, 28

Twain, Mark, 126, 137, 229

Tyler, Liv, 102, 171

Tyler, Stephen, 253

U

Unser, Al, 199

Ustinov, Peter, 12

V

Valentine, Alan, 11, 44, 87, 224

Vidal, Gore, 192, 244

von Bismarck, Otto, 103

von Schiller, Johann, 241

W

Wadsworth, Charles, 60

Walker, Rebecca, 64

Washington, Denzel, 114

Waterston, Sam, 265

Watterson, Bill, 108

Waugh, Evelyn, 30, 237

Wayans, Damon, 240

Welk, Lawrence, 132

West, Morris, xii, 276

Wiesel, Elie, 235

Wilde, Kim, 175

Wilde, Oscar, 23, 64, 127

Wilkinson, Alec, 38, 87, 235

Williams, Bern, 246

Williams, Venus, 194

Williams, William Carlos, 107, 227

Wilmot, John, 84

Wilson, Earl, 189

Wilson, Luke, 191

Wolfe, Tom, 6

Womack, Bobby, 72

Wooden, John, 230

Woods, Tiger, xi, 195

Woolf, Virginia, 161

Wordsworth, William, 6, 12

Work, Henry Clay, 66, 259

Wozniak, Steve, 215

Wright, Stephen, 249

Y

Yankovic, Al, 277

Yeager, Chuck, 204

Youngman, Henny, 240

Z

Zappa, Ahmet, 114

Zappa, Frank, 115

Zappa, Moon Unit, 172

Zemeckis, Robert, 221